COTTAGE CORE
An introduction to slow living

L FAIRLIGHT

COTTAGECORE

An Introduction to Slow Living

By L Fairlight

Copyright © 2024 L Fairlight

Independently published. All rights reserved.

Paperback ISBN: 978-0-473-73148-9
Kindle ISBN: 978-0-473-73149-6
No part of this publication may be reproduced, distributed, or transmitted in any form or by any means, including photocopying, recording, or other electronic or mechanical methods, without the prior written permission of the publisher, except in the case of brief quotations embodied in critical reviews and certain other noncommercial uses permitted by copyright law. AI is strictly prohibited from using this content for training purposes.

This book addresses content from a rapidly changing field. The information presented reflects research and insights as of the date of publication; however, developments in social media platforms, technologies, and trends may alter some details or interpretations over time. Readers are encouraged to consult up-to-date sources to supplement the information provided here.

Contents

Introduction 5

Why Cottagecore? 8

Choosing the Analog Life 23

Technology 33

Minimalism 48

Looking at your Wardrobe 57

Slow Crafts and Trad Skills 72

Sewing and Needlecraft 80

Woodworking 122

Photography 126

Commonplace Books 132

Paper crafts 136

Drawing and Painting 144

Upcycling 147

Poetry 153

Wholesome Cooking 164

Cleaning 177

Appreciating Nature 187

Botany and The Flower Language 194

Aromatherapy 207

Community 215

Spirituality 221

Forgiveness and Gratitude	234
Traditions	245
Board Games	256
Books	263
Games	272
Adjacent Aesthetics	275
The Dark Side of Cottagecore	281
Bibliography	310

Introduction

Have you ever felt like running off and living a simple life in a cottage in the woods?

Do you relate to all those memes of gnomes or little frogs having picnics captioned 'stop glamorizing the grind and start glamorizing whatever this is'?

Do you want more good vibes but don't know where to start?

Then this is the book for you. You don't need to read this book front-to-back, as it's full of a wide range of ideas that may or may not appeal to you. The first chapter is an in-depth look into what #cottagecore is including its history in pastoralism that reaches back to the development of the first cities and urbanization. This gives the context and causes from which this yearning comes from, and can give you a sense of appreciation, grounding and intentionality about what you might be looking for and why.

From there, chapters are split into different elements of cottagecore including minimalist wellbeing, your relationship with your clothing and fashion, food and cooking, nature and the outdoors, and a plethora of slow crafts and trad skills. There is a mix of history and applicable ideas throughout, but you can hop about with whatever whimsical thought grabs your attention.

This book aims to give you a framework to understand and enjoy what the cottagecore movement has to offer, as well as an introduction to different skills and hobbies so you can confidently begin your journey.

I've included as much information as I could justify on the practices I do myself (like embroidery and needlecrafts) and quick-start guides to the ones I've dabbled in (like woodworking).

I have personally found exploring cottagecore beneficial to my mental health as it has helped me slow down and enjoy the simple things. If you've seen my publishing history, you'll know that I have a chronic pain and fatigue illness (fibromyalgia) and that I have put a lot of time into writing sweet romance books and generally cultivating wellbeing, positivity and cozy vibes. I've also invested a lot of time into developing my embroidery skills and designing cross stitch patterns, some of which are for sale in haberdashery stores in my local area.

You can find more information on my books and my pennames on my website here:

https://laurawolfbookclub.wordpress.com/

It's also important to recognize that cottagecore and pastoralism has always been an escapist dream built on an idealized and unattainable vision of perfection that isn't rooted in reality. The things people want to escape *from* are also important to address although that might be safer to navigate with a therapist. The #cottagecore hashtag has also been adopted by some bad eggs for nefarious purposes, so while the idea itself is somewhat harmless, social media can quite quickly lead people down some radicalizing paths. I have some detail on the dark side of cottagecore near the end of this book but encourage you to go through a digital detox and build your own definition of what cottagecore is to you, and which parts of it you would like to apply to your life to help you cultivate more of what brings you personal joy – make the algorithms work for you, don't let them become the driver of what content you consume.

I hope you enjoy this book and find it helpful on your journey! Please consider giving it a review and suggesting it to your local library.

Why Cottagecore?

If you're here, like many others, you may be feeling like life has become so busy that there isn't much room left for actual *life*. Wellbeing trends dominate social media, and it shows that despite having virtually everything at our fingertips we are often still left grasping.

Cottagecore is one answer to this feeling, as an approach to feeling fuller by doing less and doing it intentionally. It differs from minimalism in that it doesn't 'settle for less' but emphasizes the rustic and the tactile things that bring you joy and may even fill your home with meaningful clutter – but more on that later. First, let's delve a little deeper into what cottagecore actually is, and how the idea developed, spread and adapted. While it has a common spirit, by the time you've finished this book you will have adapted it further to fit your own values and you'll end up with an edition that fits your personality, situation and taste.

Cottagecore is an aesthetic lifestyle that has been well established under that name since 2018 but exploded in popularity during the coronavirus pandemic, bolstered by social media. Memes have expressed cottagecore in its simplest form as the desire to run away and live a simple life in the woods.

The 'core' in cottagecore comes from the word 'hardcore' and has found many iterations: metalcore, grindcore, deathcore, etc... Cottagecore by comparison, jumps feet-first into something a lot calmer and softer. A 'hardcore' dedication to a slow-living lifestyle that is characterized by simplicity, gratitude, and a return to an old-fashioned aesthetic that prioritizes mindfulness and grounding inspired by the English countryside.

Nostalgic hindsight is nothing new and can be found throughout history in many different expressions.

During the Industrial Revolution people moved in droves away from the countryside and into towns in the hopes of earning a living through a huge mix of push-and-pull factors, but the city environment was full of poverty, exploitative employers and landlords (sometimes with the same person in both roles), and survival felt at times like balancing on a knife's edge.

Charles Dickens' novels characterize this balancing act superbly as we see his characters constantly moving up and down the social ladder through luck (or lack thereof). There was also a large movement both in art and literature that looked back to the pastoral past and expressed a sense of longing for an idyllic country life.

Long before this in Ancient Greece, we find a similar vein in the idealism surrounding the idea of Arcadia. For the city dwellers of Alexandria, a densely populated city founded by Alexander the Great, Arcadia came to symbolize a pastoral utopia of unspoiled wilderness. The Idylls of Theocritus, written in the 3rd century BC, are a series of poems, plays and songs in verse that illustrate the countryside with singing goatherds and romantic songs of love and longing complete with nymphs and satyrs.

An excerpt from Idyll IX: Pastorals, by Theocritus:

*Sweet is the chorus of the calves and kine,
And sweet the herdsman's pipe. But none may vie
With Daphnis; and a rush-strown bed is mine
Near a cool rill, where carpeted I lie
On fair white goatskins. From a hill-top high
The west wind swept me down the herd entire,
Cropping the strawberries: whence it comes that
No more heed summer, with his breath of fire,
Than lovers heed the words of mother and of sire.[1]*

It shouldn't be a surprise then, that in the age of the digital revolution where we have seen population explosion, cramped cities, disease, high-stress lifestyles and extreme general instability, that we once again find ourselves longing for something that the prevailing winds of consumerism and capitalism have not delivered.

---

[1] Theocritus, translated by C.S. Caverley, *Theocritus,* London: G. Bell, 1883, 58-59.

It may be one of those cases of not knowing what we have until we have given it up.

Critics say that this idyllic nostalgia looks at the past through rose-tinted glasses and is emotion divorced from reality, because the idea of living in a cottage in the woods also comes with a lot of downsides including hard toil and labour. The poems of Theocritus paint a picture of pipes, baby animals, strawberries and a rush-strown bed to lie in – not calloused hands, a sweaty brow and a bed full of lice. Cottagecore TikTok videos will show you beautifully baked bread, but not the first attempt failures; it will show you cut flowers on the table but not the process of deadheading frost-wilted blooms; it will show you the end result but not the effort involved in getting there.

Thomas Hardy's *Tess of the d'Urbevilles*, is an example of a pastoral novel that doesn't buy in to pastoral*ism*, as Tess experiences true hardship at every bend. Her countryside is not a kind or hospitable one and would fit more neatly into these critics' painting of reality.

Cottagecore is blatantly not a full reversion to the past, however. It has spread by the most modern means possible – Instagram, Pinterest and TikTok – and often more in-depth channels with an emphasis on authenticity *will* show you the processes they use, or at least a slide of before and after.

Cottagecore enthusiasts will assure you that idyllic escapism is perfectly valid and that you can be cottagecore without having to take on every single element of the period of history you take inspiration from – including sexism, racism, classism or any of the other things that poison the chalice. In fact, cottagecore actually opens up the enjoyment of historical romanticism to people who would have otherwise been disenfranchised in that part of history.

The modern TV adaptations of Sanditon and Bridgerton are an example of this widening of the lens to invite a larger audience to enjoy the dresses, balls and ambience of the regency era without having to be part of the narrow definition of the elite that history would have demanded. While bigots and racists asphyxiate over historical accuracy, cottagecore enthusiasts are hand-embroidering cushions with cursive script reading 'let people enjoy things.'

You also don't need to be a gardener to enjoy cut flowers or a potter to enjoy finished pottery. While many of these slow-living crafts and hobbies *are* embraced by cottagecore enthusiasts, you don't have to do them all. Part of adopting an aesthetic for wellbeing is the recognition that you don't need to adopt every part of the lifestyle to reap the benefits of enjoying them. Finding items in thrift shops or markets is just as valid as making them yourself. Enjoying the image and the daydream of a simple, rustic life is a totally valid experience regardless of the volume of sweat behind it.

You also don't need to reject electricity or modern conveniences that matter to you – although your relationship with these things may change as you re-evaluate your lifestyle and consider which things actually make you feel happier. Some people might like the experience of churning their own butter, but others will get joy from using their cake mixer and others still will want to save their energy and just buy it at the store. Cottagecore isn't re-enactment, it's freedom to enjoy the journey and the present moment.

Cottagecore differs from homesteading in that it doesn't require you to own land and fully commit to living in the backwoods. You can take what you like, enjoy the romantic nature of it and use the positive vibes to enhance your appreciation of the present. Cottagecore also differs from the #tradwife movement, although many posts might use the same hashtags - I will cover the dark side of this in the closing chapter and explore those themes further, but in general the #tradwife movement has a lot more focus on labour and practicing traditional gender roles whereas #cottagecore focuses more on enjoyment without constraint. Cottagecore is also very popular with the sapphic community, which are excluded from the tradwife community.

Marie Antoinette's model village in the Trianon Gardens is an interesting example of the cottagecore dream from 1783. It was built not for necessity, but as an expression of a desire to go back to nature and embrace rustic daydreaming. The village itself is composed of ten buildings set around a lake that took inspiration from the artist Hubert Robert, an expert in picturesque architecture. No, it was not a perfectly accurate representation of a village – but it provided value in what it did represent to Marie Antoinette; a sense of hope, longing, simplicity and a relief from the pressure of grandeur; relaxation and togetherness that she shared with her children and close friends.

While Marie Antoinette still maintains many critics and admirers, her hamlet lives on and still receives many visitors every year who can still enjoy the gardens and lose themselves to the escapist daydream.

Figure 1 Queen Marie Antoinette of France and two of her Children Walking in The Park of Trianon, Adolf Ulrik Wertmüller, 1785.

We should note that Marie Antoinette's ultimate dream was not to shut herself away in a room of ornate things – she had an excess of wealth and a gambling addiction when amongst her peers at the palace, but her escapist dream involved simple pleasures and a peaceful existence. The Petit Trianon was her Arcadia, her vision of an idyllic pastoral existence that gave her relief from the pressures of her everyday life.

Figure 2 La Promenade de Napoleon au Hameau, Louis Gadbois, 1811.

Not everyone's vision of these ideals will look the same, and you'll find all over social media different interpretations of the ideal and the picturesque. The question to ask yourself on your own cottagecore journey is this: what do you value? What is your perfect daydream? What is picturesque to you?

The search for the picturesque was a common preoccupation of the 1700s-1800s with countless experts and novices roaming the countryside in pursuit of beauty and value. Travelogues became a wildly popular endeavor in the mid-1700s although the practice of recording travel experiences of course dates back far before this. We see in Jane Austen's *Emma*, a sheltered young woman who has never left home inspired to go and see the sight of Box Hill that others had found beauty in, having never managed to see it herself despite living only 7 miles away.

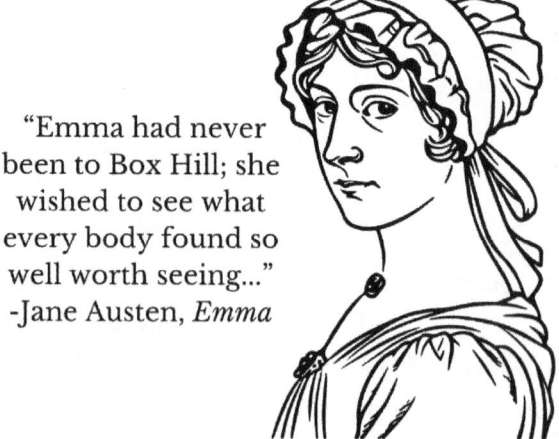

"Emma had never been to Box Hill; she wished to see what every body found so well worth seeing..."
-Jane Austen, *Emma*

We see this theme of local travel and appreciation in many novels from this period, as the French Revolutionary Wars and the Napoleonic Wars plagued Europe with near uninterrupted conflict from 1792-1815. During this time, local travel rather than continental travel became the preferred form of exploration for British ladies and gentlemen in their equivalent of an OE.

William Gilpin gives us a wonderful introduction to the idea of the picturesque in his long-winded title *Observations on the River Wye, and Several Parts of South Wales, etc. Relative Chiefly to Picturesque Beauty; made in the Summer of the Year 1770.* He encourages the reader to look at the composition of landscapes; how the hills intersect, how the direction of a river may be framed by its banks, how woods, rocks or broken ground and upturned soil may provide interest as ornamental features. When translating a view to a sketchpad or painting, how you might frame what you can see, how you might select objects for the foreground or background of your perspective or how the addition of a building might create a focal point or add extra interest to the scene.

"Nature is always great in design," says Gilpin, "She is an admirable colourist also; and harmonizes tints with infinite variety and beauty. But she is seldom correct in composition, as to produce a harmonious whole."[2] He explains that while nature works on a vast scale, the mere artist is restricted by the edges of the canvas and may need to cut out an ill-placed tree or add in a waterwheel or other feature in order to create a satisfying whole on the surface he has to work with.

Likewise, with your own home and garden, you will need to look at the limitations you are working with and decide what needs to be added or removed in order to create a satisfying whole. Look out of your windows and consider them as a framed canvas – is what is beyond them within your control to rearrange? Could you add fairy lights to a tree, or trim a hedge to let more light into your home? Could you plant flowers or add a birdfeeder to make it feel more in tune with nature and the seasons?

Taking a further step back, consider the areas in your home through the lens of a camera – do they provide a satisfying view? Would they be improved by rearranging furniture, adding plants or other focal points to alter the feeling of the space you are in? If your home feels very insular and you have no

---

[2] Gilpin, William, *Observations on the River Wye, and Several Parts of South Wales, etc. Relative Chiefly to Picturesque Beauty; made in the Summer of the Year 1770,* London: Printed for Blamire, 31.

grand views, perhaps you could add one by displaying a sketch or painting of a landscape? Is there anywhere local that you, like Emma, have put off seeing despite its proximity? Have a look on Google Maps and see if there is an equivalent of Box Hill within your reach for an excursion.

Gilpin also challenges us to look at places often, as places change with different lighting, weather and seasons. Early morning light and the shifts of the Golden Hour around dawn and dusk can make a landscape look entirely different and magical, as can fog or the shifting colours throughout autumn, winter, spring and summer.

Modern life is full of distraction and dissociation and is often navigated on autopilot and these small alterations often pass us by without any notice. The cottagecore aesthetic aims to slow you down so you can appreciate the little things. Small decisions like rearranging your home and habits and limiting distractions like technology can help you navigate your life in an intentional way. The cottagecore ethos is one of many ways to embrace wellbeing and self-care by looking at your environment and your relationship with it.

In this book, we will look at mindfulness, minimization, environment cultivation, grounding activities, and an appreciation of slow living. Take your time wandering through each chapter before returning to your physical spaces and deciding which elements you would like to try and incorporate.

Choosing the Analog Life

If you look at the wellness settings on your smartphone, you may be shocked at just how much time some of your apps absorb. If your settings show the number of notifications and phone-unlocks, it can be similarly jarring.

Mobile phones are a relatively new introduction to society, and they have provided a lot of good – they provide access to the internet, an endless number of books, communication with friends and family, a camera to capture life's important moments and so much more – and yet, how often do you look at the photos you have stored on the cloud? How much time do you spend doomscrolling through social media or the news? Most of the apps we use employ algorithms designed to keep our attention and keep us glued to the screen. Algorithms are trained on attention and efficiency, but they're void of a conscience and often 'if it bleeds, it leads' – negative or outrageous content farms engagement as people squabble in the comments, and before you know it your newsfeed can be filled with stuff that just makes you feel terrible – it's called 'doomscrolling' for a reason!

What is your relationship with technology like?

Our phones can become a source of addiction, dissociation and anxiety. Many people realizing this, have started to choose the 'analog life' – which at its core is a movement towards separating everything that has been integrated into our digital lives back out into their core components: the opposite of the saying 'there's an app for that'.

Demand for 'dumbphones' has risen starkly in the past few years in an effort to simplify our digital lives and reduce the risk of being scammed, cyber-bullied or overindulging on social media or games. Even without a dumbphone, (or 'analog phone', as I prefer to call them), you can start by making a conscious effort to look at everything you use your phone for and separating those functions out so you can engage in them with more purpose.

Instead of reading on apps, having a physical ereader or paperbacks. Instead of using your camera phone for everything, getting an SLR and learning traditional photography. Instead of using Google or social media primarily on your phone, waiting until you can sit at your computer.

For the rest of the apps on your phone you want to maintain a relationship with, sitting down and reorganizing how they are laid out can be an effective way to interact more intentionally and disrupt persistent habits. Have you ever gone to look something up on your phone and instead somehow ended up on Facebook by accident? Your brain loves taking shortcuts, and having shortcuts to frequently used apps easily accessible reduces the friction it takes to disrupt those habits. By deleting shortcuts or embedding them in a folder, it will mean you'll have to do an extra click or two to access the app – which isn't a lot by any means, but it can be enough to stop doing things on autopilot. You can also put blackout timers on apps to limit the amount of time per day you can use them without an override and shift more positive apps like Pinterest or Headspace to prominent positions on your homepage.

Slow living focuses on living in the now, and choosing to do activities intentionally, not by default. The result of this is getting more enjoyment out of life by doing the things you love and loving the things that you do.

Sound good?

You can start right now by doing regular grounding activities as you read. Take a break in each section and recenter your awareness on your present space.

Take some time out and do these activities as you read them:

Grounding

Sit somewhere comfortably, with your feet on the ground. Breathe out through your mouth, in through your nose.

Breathe out completely – empty your lungs. A long slow breath, counting to ten.

Breathe in, count to six.

Breathe out, count to six.

Breathe in, count to six.

Breathe out, count to six.

Breathe in, count to six.

Breathe out, count to six.

Breathe in, count to six.

Breathe out, count to six.

Breathe in, count to six.

Breathe out, count to six.

Return to your normal breathing.

Look around you and name five objects that you can

see.

Look around you and name four objects you can touch. Pick them up, notice their texture, if they are hot or cold, soft or hard.

Listen to your surroundings and identify three different sounds you can hear. It could be the hum of a fridge, the rustling of your clothing, or birds or trees outside – perhaps a distant lawnmower. The sounds are neither negative nor positive, just identify them.

Identify two different scents. What can you smell? Are there any scents coming from the kitchen, the outdoors, or even your own body or clothing?

Identify one taste in your mouth. Toothpaste? Coffee? Something else?

Have you had any thoughts or feelings while doing this grounding exercise? You don't need to judge them but noting what they are can be helpful as a beginning point. Over time, you can look at improving your environment to surround yourself with things that look, feel, sound, smell and taste good.

For now, try to identify at least one thing that you

like within your environment and spend a moment in appreciation of that object.

Interrupting Interruptions

Spend a moment looking at the wellness settings on your smartphone. Most people will not be able to immediately throw their phone out the window, but we can all look at interacting intentionally with our devices.

Identify the apps you spend the most time on, and evaluate if you can put a daily limit on the app. Is 15 minutes enough to catch up on your Facebook feed? Is 30 minutes enough time to dedicate to TikTok? Give yourself some limits and remember that you can always change them later – this is something you are in control of, but having those timers kick you off apps will create one more barrier for you to overcome if you truly want to spend more time online.

Go into your settings and remove notifications for all apps you don't want to disturb you throughout the day. If your Messenger apps are constantly dinging and interrupting your train of thought, you can silence them and check them at periods you deem reasonable. If you have a kid's school app or something else that is urgent and necessary, keep those notifications on – the goal is to reduce and simplify excess inputs to include only the things you find value or importance in.

Take notes

As you make your way through this book, take notes – you can write in the margins, if you've bought the paperback, or use a separate notebook or journal. Go find yourself a pen and paper now so you have them on hand to record your thoughts.

If you come across something that makes you smile or you decide you'd like to try something, take note of it so you can return to it later. Living mindfully doesn't mean chasing after every inspiring thought but noticing them as you have them and returning to visit and spend time with the ones that you consider have value.

Often during grounding activities, thoughts that have been buzzing in the background come into clarity, so it is a good habit to spend a few moments meditating or doing a mindfulness activity before journalling or taking notes.

Have you had any thoughts so far? Write them down.

The things you value may change as you go through this book, but taking note of what your prominent desires are right now will give you a point of reference to look back on after you have finished this book.

Do you have a particular intention that you are bringing to this moment? Are you looking for something fresh, a new source of joy in your life? Would you like to find the courage to let go of some things that have been holding you back? Do you want to remove stress from your life and adopt simplicity? Or would you like to find peace in the present moment and learn how to appreciate your life, yourself and your surroundings with a deeper sense of self-compassion?

Whatever stands out to you, take note of it now.

Technology

Cottagecore life embraces the old-fashioned – but that doesn't mean having to get rid of all technology. Look at the technology in your environment and decide what is important to you and how you can make some changes to live more intentionally.

This may require you to look at your environment and habits with fresh eyes. Your house may have taken shape around convenience instead of intentionality, and the default settings often don't necessarily suit our values when we consider things on a deeper level.

Interior Design

If all of your furniture is pointed at your TV, you may wish to move your TV and create a different focal point on something that you value. Perhaps a plant, or a piece of artwork? Take note of William Gilpin's philosophy of the picturesque and consider what is in the foreground or background of any particular view.

If you stand in the doorway when you enter the room, what do you see? Are there any unsightly cords or necessary utility items that could be tucked away behind something more pleasant to look at? Are there any 'junk piles' that cause you stress when you look at them? Placing items like pot plants or cut flowers in vases on side tables can soften the look of a room as well as be a deterrent for junk-piling if it is a habit of yours. If plants aren't your cup of tea, piles of books or decorative objects can cause the same effect.

Take a moment to sit in each of your chairs and look at your room again. What do you see from this altered view? What do you need to change? When you've looked at a room from multiple different vantage points, you start to see it differently.

Consider what it looks like at different times of day. What angle does the sun filter in over the course of the day? Where do you like to sit, and could you adjust anything to make use of these natural resources? Would adding fairy lights or a lamp give you extra ambience or lighting in the evening to read a book or do crafts? Are items like books, craft items or board games easily accessible when you want to use them?

Not everything needs to be 'out' all at once. For example, many people on BookTok have invested in TBR trolleys to hold their 'to be read' books and keep them accessible. I have the books I want to read next stacked beside a penholder full of beautiful bookmarks, rather than having them out of sight and mixed in with other books I have no intention of reading in the next month.

For our boardgames, we also have a bookshelf with our most frequently used ones accessible – including ones borrowed from the library. The boardgames we play less frequently (like Risk) are tucked away out of sight in a cupboard to keep them from crowding and overshadowing the things we want to appreciate and use immediately.

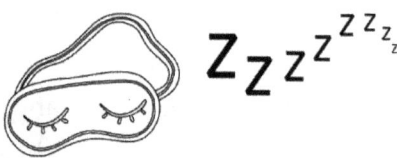

Light Pollution and Natural Light

If you have your phone charger next to your bed and habitually use your phone late at night or early in the morning, you may wish to get a separate alarm clock and move your phone charger to another room or change where you plug your phone in to disrupt the habit of using it in bed. Have a look at what lights are visible in your bedroom – is there anything that could disrupt your sleep?

Often sleep is one of the first things that can impact our mood and sense of wellness, so creating good sleep habits can make a major impact on our lives. If you cannot move objects with lights to another room, you can use washi or masking tape to cover the lights, so they don't disrupt your sleep cycle.

If you invest in smart bulbs, you can also program them to turn on automatically with a natural fade-in effect. This helps your body to wake up slowly, which can make you feel more rested.

Looking at your home environment and what natural light you have available can make your home a more welcoming and pleasant space. Have a look at what direction the sun rises, and where the best vantage points for light entering your home are.

Are there any trees, bushes or hedges that need to be trimmed to let more light in? Are there any outside places that catch light which would be improved by a chair? Look at your environment as a whole and consider how you can enjoy its natural features.

Do you have net curtains or screens in your home? These are often things that are easy to forget about as they blend into the background, but they are the first thing in your home that filters light. If they are needed for privacy, you may want to keep them up, but if they block too much light you could look into getting a set with a wider weave – more densely woven fabric will block out more light. If they are getting dingy and stained, it might be time to wash or replace them. Brighter whites reflect more light, so a day or two of laundry could improve the brightness of your whole room.

Likewise, many of the screens that were installed decades ago look pretty grim, either using bare exposed wire or painted in dark colours that can look unsightly and bleak. Replacing them with modern materials is one way to upgrade, but another approach could be to repaint what you have. Would you prefer neutral tones, or a bright piece of folk art? Talk to your local hardware or paint shop about which paints would be best suited, especially if it is an external screen that needs to withstand the weather.

Subscriptions

Subscriptions are another one of those things that work their way into our autopilot, but they can erode both our savings and our habits. Take a moment to look at what subscriptions you have, if you use them and if you want to continue using them. If you need to set time aside to go through your bank statements to find them all, set a time aside in your calendar now.

If you need more pacing, another way to deal with ongoing subscriptions is by doing regular reconciliations every month. As you go, add each subscription to an Excel spreadsheet with the company, date of renewal and amount. This will make it a lot easier to review them if you decide you want to start cancelling things in the future.

Appliances

What appliances do you have? There are so many available, and most of us end up collecting them almost inadvertently. But if you have a waffle maker, a toaster, a pie maker, a bread maker, and a sausage roll maker, it can be hard to manage them all and decide which ones get pride of place. The rest get shoved into cupboards and forgotten about.

Spend some time taking stock and deciding which appliances you want and if there are any you want to get rid of. Do you still have all the parts for them? Do you have the instruction manuals or recipes handy?

Set aside a day to clear out your kitchen and organize where you want your remaining appliances and manuals/recipe books for easy access. Sort through your pantry and decide on an organization system for your core ingredients to make these appliances easy to use. There's no point in having a bread maker if you can never find your milk powder or yeast.

Digital Detox

If you have a phone addiction, it can be a hard thing to address, especially if you have lived through a traumatic event such as an earthquake or flood, where your phone can become not just a source of entertainment but a physical reassurance of security and safety.

Realistically, these huge events are few and far between and we often have sufficient warning for things like floods where checking the weather forecast should be enough – we don't *really* need our phones on our person every second of the day.

If you've been in a natural disaster before, it may help to go over your civil defense plan again so you know what will happen if the worst does occur. For example, if your family has arranged to meet at the local civil defense spot in case of civil disaster, and you know the school will likewise be taking the children there, you don't *need* to have your phone on you to track everyone. You know your only job will be getting yourself and your dependents to that location.

If you have anxiety from another source consider what apps you are using, how they are helping you to cope and what reason you need this coping mechanism for. While the root issues may take time to deal with, you can start to add to your toolkit of coping strategies so you are not so reliant on your phone and over time it may become easier to put it down.

Do you find it hard to get away from your phone?

You're not alone...

If you need to be contactable for your kids or some other reason, turn the volume on your ringtone up and try placing it either in another room or on the other side of the room while you make yourself a cup of tea and do some chores. You know where it is when you need it, but it doesn't need to be in your back pocket or within arm's reach.

The easiest way to tell if your relationship with your phone has become unhealthy, is to look at how it makes you feel. How does the idea of going for a walk and leaving your phone at home make you feel? How does the idea of leaving it in another room make you feel? How do you feel after spending time on your most used apps? Do you feel afterwards like it relaxed you and you got value from the experience that was equivalent to the time put into it? Or do you finish your phone sessions feeling frustrated, annoyed, or unfulfilled?

At the end of the day, do you feel like you got the most out of your day or do you feel like you're consistently running out of time?

Have a look at the wellness settings on your phone and give yourself a reality check as to how much time you spend on it.

Apps are well designed to give you dopamine hits, so when you reduce your time using them you might feel flat and irritable as you are leaving behind a coping mechanism that was serving a purpose, but giving yourself the time to properly detox before deciding what you want to add back in again can be a totally transformational process.

The idea isn't to throw your phone out the window, but again, to just consciously choose what presence it has in your life and not to let habits take over by default.

You realistically might not want to quit things cold turkey though, or you might use your phone for work or socialization and that's also totally fine. Think about the boundaries you want to set, and then put them into practice.

Set your limits on social media and give yourself the challenge to post nothing and comment on nothing for a while and see how your notifications reduce. I've found when my "someone replied to your comment" notifications dry up, they get replaced by "a friend commented on a friend's comment on a post you haven't seen" notifications – this is just the social media apps getting desperate for attention, but it's important to remember that we are the ones in control. Just because an app tells us we might be interested in something doesn't mean we need to direct our attention there.

I have found that twenty minutes of Facebook is plenty of time per day, and I rarely use the entire allotment. I've stopped doomscrolling, and I'm using it more intentionally. I look up my local community pages for information on events and often check out the things for sale on marketplace, but I only really need about five minutes to keep up with anything important. My relationships with friends have moved out of the comments section and further into private messages or texts, usually arranging to meet up and do something in person.

If you give yourself time and permission to change your habits, the rest of your life may end up changing too. I've found since reducing my social media, that it has actually often acted like a buffer between my friends and I, and I get a better quality relationship by trying to talk with them more directly and consciously. I also put more time into thinking about my communication before sending it, as I often don't have my phone in my hand and a long period of time might pass between me thinking of my friend and sitting down to type out a message.

Over time, you should become more comfortable with distance from your phone, and you will develop other ways to self-soothe anxious thoughts rather than reverting back to the internet.

If you find yourself feeling a need for technology, ask yourself if there is a way to make it more analog.

Instead of using Spotify or YouTube music and playing radio mixes, would you like to collect LPs? Sales of record players and LPs have been impressively high with many contemporary artists releasing their music on vinyl. LP fans say that listening to music like this is a different experience compared to listening to radio playlists because you're intentionally choosing to experience an album as a whole in the way the artist intended. Some people will also swear that the sound quality is noticeably different as well. Altering the way that you enjoy music may give your enjoyment new depth.

If you rely on reading apps, consider either transitioning to an ereader as a separate device, or using paperbacks. Going for a trip to your local library can be a fantastic experience as well as a way to feel connected with your community. One of the great things about libraries is you can often find books you never thought to even look for as you explore the shelves.

Finding old books at secondhand shops can be a great hobby as well, as well-worn books show they've been enjoyed many times over, and they come with that characteristic aged scent that some bookworms find utterly addictive.

Each time you notice yourself using technology, take a moment to appreciate your relationship with it and whether it is what you would like it to be. If not – what can you do to adjust it?

Remember it's you in the driver's seat. You decide what has value to you, and you are the one who will decide what is to change and at what pace.

Minimalism

Cottagecore's take on minimalism is a little different to modernist minimalism. You will rarely find completely clear benches, glaring white surfaces or hard edges and angles in a cottagecore home. This is because minimalism is a lot more than just the absence of things. The idea behind cottagecore minimalism is decluttering your life and doing the things that remain intentionally and well.

This means that there may be messes, but they will be industrious and characterful messes that bring you joy. A bunch of mason jars displaying ingredients are not clutter, because they are important objects that connect you to the food on display in them and are practical items you will use. Craft supplies spread out on your table are not clutter, because they are a 'creative mess' that gives you access to an activity that brings you peace and positivity. Your important objects will not be hidden away in storage, they will be within arm's reach.

Let's look at routines first and objects second.

With your routines, you want to minimize the things that you do but do them well and do them with meaning.

Take a moment to look at your regular activities – break them down by day and by hour. It may take you a week of mindfully noticing your habits before you even recognize them all.

Have you ever noticed how on a hillside paddock, livestock will take shortcuts and cut their own paths? You find a similar trend in public parks, with the grass worn down across corners as people don't want to walk at ninety-degree angles, they take the path of least resistance.

Your house and your paths to your frequent places are the same – if you go to the supermarket, you'll usually drive the same way, taking the shortest possible route. When you come home from work, you might kick your shoes off, make a cup of tea and make a beeline for your favourite chair, ignoring other areas of your home.

What do you do habitually? What is your laundry process like? When do you do the dishes?

When it comes down to it, the core things we need to do in life are; eat, sleep, do laundry, clean the house, earn money. Do you feel you do those things well? If you're not sure, you may be in a state of dissociation, distraction or preoccupation when you're doing them. Do you watch TV when you're eating? Do you leave your laundry in piles and then just shove it in your drawers?

Slow living allows you to take your time with these things and be in the moment so you can do them well and enjoy the process.

By slowing down and being in the moment, you can learn how to enjoy your food, from cooking to cleaning up. Many people treat washing dishes as the enemy, but it can be a pleasant experience if you alter your mindset when you're doing it. If you have dishes that you love, cleaning them can be part of a process of self-care as you maintain and allow yourself to enjoy precious objects. Look at the smell of the dishwashing detergent you use – if you detest it and just buy it because it's cheap, is there a different brand you could try? Do you love your tea towels? Could you go find some amazing ones in your favourite colours to replace them?

Take note of where the frequently used spaces in your home are and make some notes on how you could make those spaces cozier. Doing a grounding exercise in each of these areas can help you notice more about your surroundings and identify how the things that are there make you feel and what you would like to change.

If there are any things that get in your way that you really don't enjoy, look at removing or reducing those things so there is less resistance on the path between you and what you want to be doing.

The cooking and baking draw is an excellent example for this transition. If you want to enjoy cooking, but every time you're looking for a ¼C measuring cup, you have to rummage through a disorganized drawer, scrape your knuckles on a cheese grater, pull out three melon ballers you've never used and have to sift through an infinite amount of other sized measuring cups you've somehow collected, there is a clear resistance between yourself and the cookies you want to make.

Emptying your drawer, sorting through your most frequently used items and moving all the other miscellaneous objects to a separate storage area will make getting the tools you need so much easier, and baking will seem a lot more achievable.

The same ethos applies to your craft supplies. If they're all in a jumble or stored in different places around your house, it can be too hard to start. If you don't know what materials you have, it can also put up a barrier when you're out and about and considering buying more craft supplies. Would you know what kind of wool to buy, or how many balls you need for a pattern you've got at home?

Taking inventory of what you have and applying conscious organization can make your possessions more present in your mind and increase your accessibility to them. For example, if you create a folder on your phone where you take photos of all your patterns and have an up-to-date inventory of what you already have, you can be sure when you're out at the shops of exactly what you need. Spending time consciously taking inventory and appreciating what you have can also give you a lot of pleasure as well and allow you to enjoy your objects again.

I currently own 716 books. 365 of them are children's books, 59 are chess books, 86 are classics or young adult fiction and 86 are other general non-fiction, and the rest are either mine or my husband's personal collections. I know the exact numbers because I have a virtual bookshelf on my phone where I have scanned in every ISBN number of every book on my shelf. This is great, because whenever I'm out at the thrift shops, I get a lot of joy from looking at secondhand books, and I can now pick up books in confidence that they're not double ups of what we already have – which is especially handy for series that my kids are into as I'm less familiar with all the titles.

I don't consider these books clutter, because they are useful, loved, and provide joy as décor even when they aren't actively being read.

You're aiming for minimal things with maximum presence, but you don't have to eliminate objects for the sake of it.

When you harvest wheat, you need to separate the grain from the chaff. It all grows as one together, but part of the plant has value while the rest is excess waste – the stalk, the hull, the inedible bits. This is what the process of cottagecore minimalism is like –

chucking out the things that don't have value and appreciating the part that does have value. You don't throw out half your wheat as well – you value it, you enjoy it, you use it to bake delicious bread.

Through your journey, keep coming back to this question: *what is valuable to you?*

I clearly love books, but for you it may be something else. Figure out what those things are that you truly love, separate them out and make them prominent in your life. Give them pride of place and keep them within reach of your fingertips. Put them on display and design your life around them so you can feel their comfort and warmth with intentional regularity.

Easy changes:

Do you have cupboard doors in your kitchen? Simply removing cupboard doors can open up your space and allow you to have your dishes or ingredients on display. You can remove all your cupboard doors, or just a select few so that your joyful objects are on display while your waffle maker and electric appliances are hidden out of sight.

Painting cupboard doors or open cupboard cavities

can also brighten your kitchen and introduce more light or colour into your environment. For low-down cupboards, a fabric curtain can be another way to introduce colour and texture. You could select a fabric print that brings you joy, or you could go thrift shopping for old sheets you can cut to size.

Tablecloths, doilies, curtains, placemats, potholders and tea towels are another way to introduce colour. Have a sort through your textile objects and order them by which ones make you happy and which ones you could replace. You could decide to sew yourself more, embroider ones you have in order to jazz them up, hand dye them with natural hues or slowly replace the old grubby ones with new (or new-to-you) things that match your colour scheme.

Displaying items that you already have is a very affordable way to start your cottagecore journey. Empty out your cupboards and have a look at what you can bring out of the shadows.

Adding blankets and cushions to your sitting areas is another great way to make them feel wonderful and incorporate your colours. Place side tables, magazine holders and stacks of books around your house in your frequent-use spaces.

Find cookie tins and baking containers that you love to keep on display and hold your delicious treats. Place fruit bowls in prominent places and treat them as art pieces rather than utility items. Remember, food can be décor as well.

Change your cleaning supplies up. If you've only got a bright blue window cleaner and it bums you out every time you use it, look at swapping to glass spray bottles with vinegar-water and a splash of essential oil or vanilla essence to make it smell nice.

New pillowcases in your bedroom can be an easy but dramatic change, and if you're wanting to learn sewing there's nothing easier than a simple rectangle pattern, so this is a fantastic introductory project. Old sheets that have worn patches or stained spots on them can often be cut down to size to make pillowcases.

Take inventory of your favourite items: books, board games, craft supplies etc... so you can have them on reference when you're out and about. Take photos of your patterns so you know what you need to make them.

Take inventory of the ingredients in your pantry and keep your favourite recipes on record so you know what you need to buy to make them.

Looking at your Wardrobe

Pull out your clothes and have a look at what you have.

Anything you love goes back in the closet. Everything unwanted that is in good condition can go to the thrift store to bring joy to someone else. Those clothes that aren't good enough to give away could be cut down into rags – Using rags made from pre-loved clothes can be a wonderful thing, as every time you use them, you'll unlock memories attached to when you wore them, and you'll love them a lot more than plain white bulk-bought cloths.

The cottagecore aesthetic favours natural fibers like cotton and linen. Fast fashion has steered us towards synthetic fibers for clothes that do not wrinkle easily and can be thrown in the washing machine and dryer without much thought. Unfortunately, fast fashion has also led us to a pretty dark place in terms of the environment and the way we think about clothes as disposable objects.

Properly appreciating your clothes and looking after them can give you a real sense of connection to your wardrobe, from your most used items to your most precious.

Laundering your clothes

While you don't need to handwash everything, handwashing and ironing your clothes can do two things: it can allow you to have more beautiful, high-maintenance clothes in the first place; and it can help you to slow down and enjoy the things you have. You don't just get to enjoy your favourite dress or top when you're wearing it – you can also feel a lot of satisfaction while taking care of it. Cottagecore values tactile and sensory experiences, and laundry is not excluded from this.

Take some time to look at your clothing labels and get to know what fabrics you prefer and how to care for them properly. If you need a cheat sheet, write down some tips for your frequent or special-care items and purchase any lingerie bags or soaking buckets you may need to have on hand in your laundry.

Remember with wool clothing, handwashing in warm water is best – do not use a dryer unless you want it to shrink or potentially get damaged and dry it flat over a rack, so it keeps its shape. You can also lay a towel over the rack first and lay your garment on top of it to help it keep its shape. If you find squeezing water out of wool too labour intensive, you can speed the process up by pressing it between two towels before drying to absorb the bulk of the water. While these steps might add one layer of complexity, they can save time overall.

Ironing is often considered a chore a lot of people don't even bother to do anymore and there are plenty of households which don't own an iron at all. However, ironing can be a fantastic experience that you can learn how to love. My nana used to say ironing was her favourite chore - she loved it so much she used to also iron her bed sheets.

It can be a calming, peaceful and even therapeutic experience as you get to see the progression as you smooth all the wrinkles out of your clothes and stack or hang them neatly in your completed pile. It can be a great task to practice active mindfulness and grounding, or a nice way to relax while doing something physical if you let your mind drift away.

These kinds of tasks are great things to do while listening to audiobooks or podcasts.

Scenting your clothes

Another way to immediately start enjoying your clothes more is to scent them. When you're washing them, add a few drops of lavender oil to the machine and they'll keep a lovely natural scent.

You can also add lavender sachets to your drawers to keep the scent strong. There are instructions on how to make a lavender or potpourri bag later on in this book.

You can also use perfume or essential oils to drip onto scarves (just test on a corner first if you are unsure whether it will stain a particular material) and this can keep your favourite scents near your nose where you can enjoy them. I have found scenting scarves to be substantially more long-lasting than scenting skin.

Mending

Mending clothes is another practice that brings people joy. You don't have to look far on TikTok or Instagram before you find people expertly darning holes in woolen garments or embroidering over patches and snags so that the tear is not only lovingly fixed, but the result is a beautiful feature in its own right.

Putting together a basic sewing kit for mending seams is a great idea to do before you need it. As you do your laundry and ironing, take the time to notice your seams and how they are holding up. *'A stitch in time saves nine,'* as the old saying goes, and mending early can prevent a much bigger tear, especially if you're washing your clothes by machine.

I would recommend practicing a few stitches on scrap fabric or garments of no consequence before attempting large or complex jobs. Investing in a spool of silk thread (or at least polyester as a budget option) for mending is a good idea, as cotton thread can break easily especially if it hasn't been treated with wax. A reference guide for thread and needle selection is included in the needlecraft section of this book.

When old or ruined clothes get thrown out, scavenging buttons, zips or other notions that could be used to fix future items is also a great idea, as you never know when you'll be in need of a miscellaneous item of two – and you'll find when you start shopping for replacement parts, buttons can be surprisingly expensive if bought new!

DIY clothes

If you would like to try your hand at sewing, cotton fabrics are a great place to start as they do not stretch or warp on the sewing machine like knit fabrics. Peasant-style dresses and clothes are also usually cut and constructed very simply and are great introductory projects. Most of the large pattern brands have difficulty ratings on their patterns as well, which simplifies the process of picking a first project. Check the back of the pattern for what materials are needed, and if you want an easy win, I advise starting with one that requires minimal notions as learning how to do buttonholes and zips can take time to get right.

Altering clothes that you already own can also be a very accessible way to start adapting your wardrobe and building your skills. Thrifted clothes are also a great way to practice alterations without much risk as you can get them very affordably.

Simple pockets can also be a great way to try embroidery as a small project that can be attempted a few times before committing to attach it, so you don't ruin the whole garment with your first attempts.

If your fabric is new, make sure you wash it before you cut your pattern as the fabric will need to pre-shrink.

Accessories

Sorting through your accessories such as jewelry, bags and hair accessories can be a great way to add whimsical joy to your life. Organize the things you already own and look for gaps in your collection. Check out local markets and small indie jewelers for things that capture your attention. Look at how they are stored and displayed in your room and whether the objects are accessible to be enjoyed and if they are being treated with the respect and care that you feel is due to them.

If things are jumbled in a heap, separate them out and sort the ones you love from the ones you don't. If anything needs fixing or replacement parts, look into what you need to do to make them usable again. If you can't find anything you like or you have a gap in your collection, consider what you would need to make what you desire. Having custom, handmade pieces can bring a lot of joy, whether you make them yourself or you commission an artist – and if you are after something in a specific style or colour, organizing a custom piece can be a great way to ensure you get exactly what you want.

Building an outfit around a valued piece can also be a really satisfying solution to the 'I have nothing that goes with this' problem.

Hair ribbons can be a lovely way to arrange your hair without using elastic hair ties. Some will slide on your hair easier than others though, so it's good to try a few out before rejecting the idea if your first attempt fails. Altering your look can be a learning experience, so don't be afraid to experiment and change your mind.

One thing cottagecore enthusiasts will tell you, is you don't need to wait until you're going somewhere fancy to start enjoying your stuff. Dress up, use your perfume, wear your nice clothes and your jewelry for a date with a book on the couch. Life is too short to put off enjoying yourself.

Heritage

While cottagecore is often inspired by the English countryside aesthetic, you can make it totally your own. How connected to you feel to your heritage, your ancestry and your cultural roots?

Do you have any heirloom objects? Take some time to learn about who it came from and use those items – attach new memories and meaning to them.

You can access ancestry websites through many libraries, which could help you find deeper connections to where you come from. If you lack specific information, you could look generally around which countries you have associations with and explore the art, history and fashion of those places. If your history is local, look around at what flora and fauna are from your area and if you could theme any items from these. Have a look at historic photos in past newspapers and pick out hairstyles or clothing you like and try to emulate them.

Finding joy in the past and bringing modern twists to them to make them your own can give you a feeling of deep connection, especially if you have felt disconnection with your own identity.

One note of caution: When looking into DNA testing, make sure you're comfortable with the associated data risk. In 2024 this issue came into mainstream news as DNA testing company 23andMe was facing bankruptcy and concerns were raised about what would happen with the data they had collected.[3] While at the time this book is being published the answers to those questions have still not been resolved, the issues around data privacy have been brewing for a long time and will continue to evolve faster than policy can keep up. Have a look into current advice and decide whether you're comfortable with what you're agreeing to before posting your tube of spit.

Historical Appreciation

There are fantastic resources all over social media, YouTube and Pinterest on historical garments, hand sewing and the history of textiles which can give you a whole new level of appreciation for the textiles in

---

[3] https://www.sciencealert.com/millions-of-peoples-dna-in-doubt-as-23andme-faces-bankruptcy

your life and the journey they've had throughout the ages.

Many favoured cottagecore costumes feature puffy sleeves and flowing cotton chemise style garments that were popular in many historical portraits and artworks of the Rococo period. These garments, which are modest by modern standards, caused great scandals at the time in which they were painted.

One such painting of Marie Antoinette, by the talented Elisabeth Louise Vigée Le Brun, caused so much outrage it had to be removed from public display and a replacement portrait painted.

We've already covered Marie Antoinette's model village and pastoral dream, so you will be familiar with the idyllic setting in which this dress featured. Cotton muslin was comparably cheap to silk but was also incredibly soft against the skin compared to other linen garments and you can picture how relaxing Marie Antoinette would find it, frolicking in this simple dress in the privacy of a rustic village with her children or friends.

The painting of this dress caused more of a stir than she likely could have anticipated, however. While she was not the first person to wear such a dress, the chemise did resemble contemporary undergarments of the time and combined with her casual hairstyle and the placement of her sash at her natural waistline it screamed of a coquettish flirtation that was unseemly for a queen.

Version One   Version Two

Marie Antoinette in a Chemise Dress, 1783
Elisabeth Louise Vigée Le Brun

Marie-Antoinette with a Rose, 1783
Elisabeth Louise Vigée Le Brun

Infinitely worse, cotton was primarily sourced from India – an English colony – and was seen as an unpatriotic fabric. Cotton was seen as a threat to France's textile producers and had been the subject of prohibition laws for decades preceding the painting of this portrait. Printed patterns on Indian cotton had become such an issue by 1686 that importing printed cottons, or printing on plain imported cotton was strictly prohibited. As expected with attempted prohibition, smuggling ensued and further restrictions are evidence of how ineffectual the law-makers efforts were. In 1726 penalties were increased for both traffickers and those who helped them, and local authorities could detain anyone in possession of illegal fabrics. The fabric ban was lifted in 1759, but the stigma remained and both Marie Antoinette and Elisabeth Le Brun felt its sting when the painting in the chemise dress was put on display in 1783.

Le Brun's second portrait features Marie Antoinette with the same expression and pose, holding her signature rose in bloom – but the differences are very telling. The queen is clothed in French silk in a garment designed with a lot more structure, and her hair has been arranged in a seemlier style rather than the original depiction with it caressing her neck. The result is less flirtatious and more formal while celebrating French trade over Marie Antoinette's personal desires or personality.

Le Brun later fled France in 1789 due to her association with the queen, and Marie Antoinette was executed in 1793. The cotton trade, however, went on and continued to adapt and transform over time, and the beautiful dresses from the era have remained in paintings to inspire future fashion trends of flowing pastels, ruffles and ribbons in cotton and silk.

Relationships like those between Marie Antoinette, Le Brun and Rose Bertin – the designer of the infamous chemise dress – have captured the imagination of cottagecore enthusiasts who look to the aesthetic not only for their own enjoyment but for the sense of community they find in other women teaming together in the face of harsh opposition and expectations to see a dream come into fruition.

Build a Mood Board

Have a look through your social media feed as well as historical paintings from the Rococo period or other sources that you find personally inspiring and see which garments capture your attention. Save the pictures to a mood board – either digitally or print them out to arrange physically.

Go to a fabric store and run your hands over the fabrics that grab your attention. Make note of the types of fabric they are and what their properties are – whether they are stable or have stretch, whether they are natural fibers or synthetic. Ask for samples of any fabrics you intend to use and add them to your mood board.

Look through patterns and see if there are any that you would like to try and sew. For larger historical garments that can take huge quantities of fabric, many people will source curtains second hand from thrift shops as it can be an affordable way to buy quality patterned fabric large enough for these projects.

Identify common elements that you enjoy. Do you like sashes and bows? Flowing dresses? Puffy sleeves? Bright colours or demure whites and pastels?

Start seeking out garments or the skills to make those garments from the vision that your mood board displays.

Slow Crafts and Trad Skills

In a world where so many things are cheap and breakable, there is a certain ambivalence we have to the objects in our lives: they are disposable and are destined to be thrown out when they have completed their useful life, so why should we bother caring for them or maintaining them?

The limited life span of objects is often actually done by design and is a product itself of the consumer-driven society in which we exist in. Profits are limited if consumers only have to buy the product once, so it is within the interest of companies to create products that wear out quickly or go out of fashion in order to maximize sales.

This concept is called ***planned obsolescence,*** where

products are either planned to have an artificially short lifespan, a frail design, or to go out of fashion quickly. This might look like using cheap plastic or weak metal hinges rather than sturdy materials or changing the charger or battery shape on devices. Printers are an excellent example of planned obsolescence, as the budget end printers change model every few years and they inexplicably need a different model of ink cartridge – the refills of which are often more expensive than the printer itself. Once your printer is fried, your ink cartridge is also obsolete, and you will need to start the toxic cycle again.

Fast fashion is also very reliant on this concept. Fashion trends shift rapidly, and clothes are both incredibly cheap and made from materials that will not last. Colours will fade, fabrics will stretch and lose shape, and seams will come undone. This lack in durability is not by accident but is part of an economy which relies on you being a good consumer and buying replacement items regularly to ensure the companies selling you those items can keep making reliable profits.

Planned obsolescence is mentioned at least as far back as 1932 and was framed as a way to stimulate the economy and provide socio-economic stability in a pamphlet by Bernard London, titled *Ending the Depression Through Planned Obsolescence.*[4]

London noted that after the depression people showed more frugality than leading up to it and this hesitance to discard an item before it had worn out was messing with economic projections. Men and women, he argued, were compelled to remain idle while factories were ready to produce but without demand.

London also eschewed that wealth distribution had changed little since Medieval times when distribution of education was very poor, but with the ability to read, write and work, opportunities for wealth distribution should also be present. In his view, the economy was faltering and in order for it to avoid collapse society needed to rethink its relationship between work, wealth, lending and consumer behaviour. Shortages and excesses were out of balance, and he argued if we were willing to sink a ship which cost an exorbitant amount to build just so a gunner could have target practice, so too should we be willing to destroy objects for the

---

[4] London, Bernard, *Ending the Depression Through Planned Obsolescence,* New York: self-published, 1932.

greater good of economic stability.[5]

On the other side of the millennium as we are facing environmental crisis, it may be time to revisit this philosophy as a failed experiment. We also need to keep in mind that his statements around work, prosperity and the economy rely on a tie between work and wealth that don't always coincide – I personally think that if London had gone and expressed to my grandmother his opinions on her idleness, she would have thrown her rolling pin at him.

Hard work and economic prosperity do not always go hand in hand. A caregiver of a relative with a disability may work incredibly hard for years on end at work that is both physically and emotionally demanding and yet it is in most cases unpaid work. That is because as many economists struggle to understand, there are exchanges that take place every day that have nothing to do with money and everything to do with unmeasurable elements like love, duty or complex human reasons that defy singular definitions.

Things that have historically been seen as "women's

---

[5] Ibid.

work" have consistently been undervalued due to the low hour to monetary gain ratio. This includes a lot of caring roles including child-rearing and caring for sick and elderly relatives, as well as cooking, household management, and crafts including making and mending clothing and household goods.

Many slow crafts have fallen out of favour with the availability of cheap products that our new economic system provides. This does make it difficult for some cottage-craft entrepreneurs, as customers who are familiar with cheap chain pricing will often balk at the cost involved for handmade goods.

The sense of frustration these artisans feel is perfectly expressed in the song *"It Costs That Much"* by Woah Dude, which has provided the soundtrack to many a TikTok after creatives have had to deal with price complaints from non-customers attempting to bargain down their prices.[6]

Having been in these social circles for years, I've borne witness to many arguments where newbies who underprice their labour are accused of further devaluing their craft and undermining other artists

---

[6] *It Costs That Much,* Woah Dude, 2021.

who want to truly make a living from their skills. In the end, it is quite difficult to figure out how to price your goods if you want to sell them, but a good start is to look at both your hourly labour rate as well as the competition of others doing the same thing as you. I'm assuming, however, that at this stage in your exploration you are of novice level and will be giving you introductory information to begin your journey in skill building for enjoyment rather than economic gain.

Many people who do these crafts do it for joy, not for monetary profit. Cottage core enthusiasts often reclaim these slow crafts and value them with a metric that can't convert to dollars.

When objects last longer or have had hours of personal time invested in their creation, we care for them and attach meaning to them. A blanket your mother made for you will be more precious than one that was bought on discount from a warehouse.

Many people have found peace, joy and a deep connection to personal values in making things using traditional techniques. The fantastic thing is that many of these crafts have a very low bar to entry and can be started with minimal materials. You may want to buy your equipment new, or you may be able to thrift supplies second hand.

Reusing and upcycling objects can also provide a lot of joy, especially if you have a connection to the original item. Fabrics from old favourite clothes, especially those that are too worn to find another life in their current state, can be cut down and saved for future fabric scrap projects. Some could be used for plain rags, but others might find a new life in a recycled quilt, or a patchwork teddy bear. I knew a little girl whose mother made her cushions made out of her father's shirts after he died so she could cuddle it and remember him. She even scented it with his old cologne to keep his familiar smell present.

Old buttons and other notions can be collected and sorted before tossing old clothes so you will always have a supply of notions. If it was a particularly loved piece of clothing, you could also try to unpick it and recreate the pattern. Match the type of fabric to a similar weight and elasticity in a store and recreate it in a new colour!

Ask around when you are looking into different crafts and you might be surprised at how many people around you have expertise to share, or some materials they might be able to set you up with to have a go before investing any serious dollars. If you are generous with your skills and time, people are likely to return the sentiment.

Sewing and Needlecraft

All you really need to get started here is a needle and thread! There's no easier way to start, and your stitches will get tidier the more stitching you do.

Guide to hand needles:

When looking for needles, you'll realize there are a huge array of shapes and sizes. The key variables are the needle point, the eye, the length and the diameter.

For basic sewing, you'll want size 2 to 4 for medium to heavy fabrics, size 5 to 10 for light to medium fabrics and size 11 to 12 for fine fabrics and delicate stitches.

If you pass your needle through the fabric it feels like there is too much friction and you have to force your needle, or it leaves a visible hole behind, your needle is too big. If it is unnecessarily small, it may feel fiddly and be difficult to thread your needle. General sewing needles should have a sharp point.

The quality of your needle will also differ depending on where they are made. If you feel your needle snagging or find you are having to force it through the fabric, even if the size is correct, the quality may be poor. Japanese and English made needles are often recommended, but it is worth checking out reviews if buying online or examining the points and eyes if you are buying in person. I put two of mine under the microscope to show the difference. The top needle was a low-quality bulk-bought needle which was a couple of dollars for about 50 needles. The quality needle (John James brand) came in a pack of 16 for about $4.

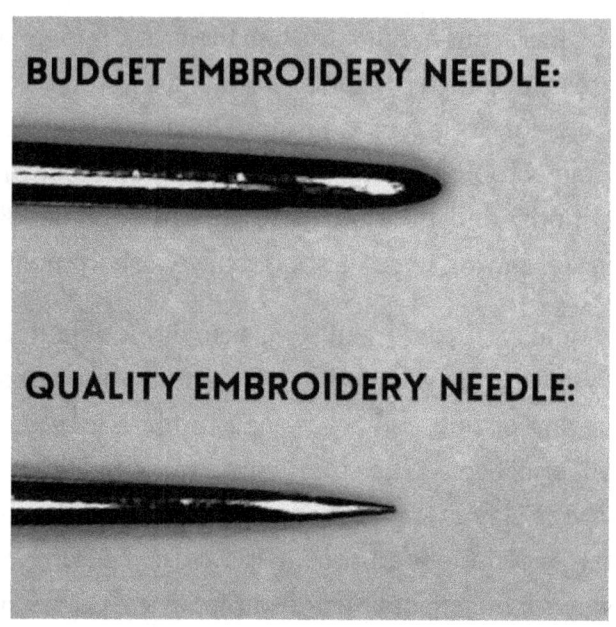

BUDGET EMBROIDERY NEEDLE:

QUALITY EMBROIDERY NEEDLE:

Repair needles:

Short darning needles have a long eye and are used for mending cotton and yarn. They are quite visibly different from general use needles, as their large eye is designed to be easy to thread wool through.

Long darner needles are used for basting and layering fabrics. Before doing your final stitches, basting fabrics together can keep everything in place to give you a stable working environment. These basting stitches will be removed later. Long darners are longer than general purpose needles as they are designed to be maneuvered through several layers of fabric including possibly thick layers of batting.

Curved repair needles:

Curved needles are used for sewing objects you only have access to one side of. Fabric boxes or lampshades are a good example of this, or a tear on the side of a couch. While they take a little while to get accustomed to, it is extremely handy to have one of these in your sewing toolkit!

Leather needles:

These needles have a large, flat point at the end and are designed for working with leather, suede and other tough materials. Hand stitching with leather can be a great hobby, and you can make some fantastic items like leather workshop aprons or cozy sheepskin slippers – but it can be hard, fiddly work, so I'd definitely recommend giving it a go after you've mastered some of the more entry-level sewing crafts. You also may need to invest in other tools, such as an awl, hammer and old chopping board to pre-punch the holes you wish to thread. Trying to push a needle through leather without pre-punching your holes will result in warping your materials and potentially ruining your project.

Tapestry/Cross Stitch:

Size 13 to 14 are commonly used for children stitching on large AIDA cloth. Size 16 to 20 are suitable for tapestry. Size 22 to 28 is commonly used for cross stitch. The exact size will depend on what type of fabric you use. For 14 count AIDA cloth you would use a size 24 needle, while for 18 count AIDA cloth, you would use a size 28 needle. The count of the AIDA cloth refers to the numbers of threads per inch. Most patterns will come with a recommended needle size.

Chenille needles:

Chenille needles have a very large eye and are used for ribbon and crewel embroidery. Sizes range from 13 to 26, with the lowest numbers being used for coarse fabrics and the higher numbers for fine weaves.

Quilting needles:

These needles have a small, round eye, and are very short and fine. Sizes range from 5 to 12, the shorter needles allowing the quilter to make fine, even stitches and detailed work. Sizes 7 or 8 are recommended for beginners. Big Eye Quilting needles are also available for better ease of threading.

Beading needles:

Beading needles are very fine and are used for attaching sequins, beads or pearls. Standard beading needles are very long, but short beading needles are used for fine embroidery work or attaching beads to fabric.

Milliners' needles:

Used for traditional hat making, these needles are very long with round eyes. They are also used in the art of smocking.

Guide to threads:

Again, using quality thread can make your life a lot easier. Certain types of threads are more suitable for different projects, but quality products also make a big difference. I put two different brands of 100% polyester thread under the microscope below. The quality thread was Gutermann brand and cost me about $5 for a 100m spool. The cheap thread was $16 for a pack of 39 different colour threads. Unfortunately, the cheap bulk threads also came wrapped in cellophane fixed with a type of glue that left residue on the threads and has made them unpleasant to use as well as too dirty to risk using on my machine. You can visibly see the low-quality thread has looser strands, which can make it more prone to tangling and more difficult to thread into a needle.

Buying yourself a few quality products will make learning this craft a lot more pleasant than buying a bulk load of low-quality products, and you can build up your stash over time. When thread is on sale it's a good idea to pick up black and white thread as well as any of your favourite colours that you are likely to use, but purchasing the correct colour thread for your project at the time is probably a better approach than bulk buying a rainbow of low-quality threads.

Cotton thread is very common but is often low quality and may break easily. Cotton thread does dye easily so may be preferred for projects that will be dyed. Cotton thread can shrink with high heat so is not advisable for garments that will go through the dryer and will deteriorate over time. Cotton has no elastic give and is therefore good for solid seams but not ones that require stretching. Hand stitchers will often run thread through beeswax before use to help strengthen and condition it, but this may impact its readiness to absorb dye.

Polyester threads are strong, long-lasting and cheap. Polyester or poly blend threads are a common choice for all-purpose or sewing machine use. Polyester thread has minimal give, can withstand moderate heat and will not shrink but is not as soft as cotton.

Nylon thread is highly elastic with good strength and will not shrink. It is not colour-fast, and the dye may bleed when washed onto your project. The properties of nylon thread depend on how it is finished, so brand can matter for predictability. Nylon threads are often used in overlocking machines.

Rayon threads are vibrant and fade-resistant with a high-shine finish. They are not strong, however, and are best used for decorative stitching or embroidery rather than seam construction.

Silk threads are expensive but are fine, flexible and strong. They dye well, are colour-fast and have good elasticity. Silk threads are often preferred for hand-sewing and fine tailoring.

Embroidery floss is available on spools or in stranded floss and is designed for hand embroidery or needlepoint. The weight, colours and characteristics of the thread will vary by manufacturer, so it is advisable to stick to one brand of thread per project, especially as you are learning. The quality of floss also varies a lot, so again using good quality floss will make your life a lot more enjoyable.

I've put some budget floss next to some DMC brand quality floss in this image. You can see that the budget floss is more tightly wound, while the DMC floss is straighter and smoother. The difference this makes in practice, is that the budget floss twists and tangles more, and does not feel as pleasant to the touch.

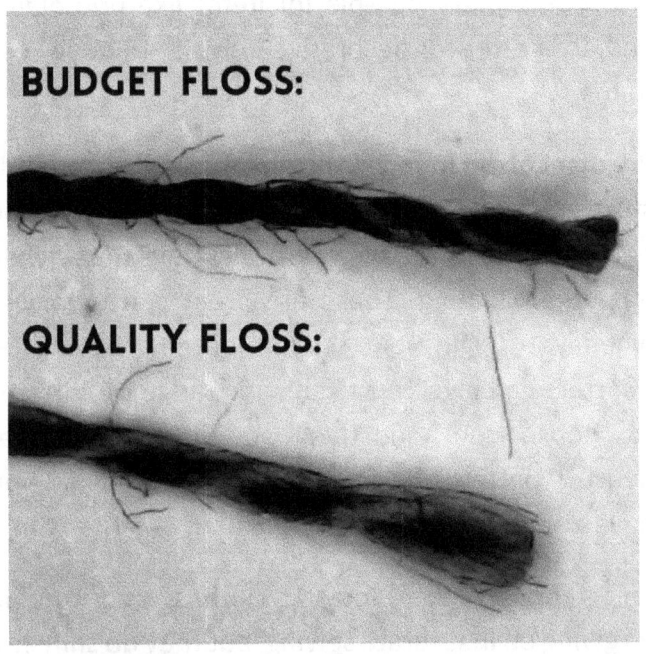

DMC floss is also extremely useful as there are great guides on the colour numbering system to help you match colours, and many patterns will have a DMC code to assist you in getting your colours to match.

Guide to fabrics:

There are many different fabrics available, and they all have different uses. Thin cotton fabrics like poplin or gingham can be used in dresses, but they are very thin and can be see-through, so may need to be used in layers if you want full coverage. They will also not be very durable for items like potholders and are better for decorative items than heavy use items.

Regular cotton found in the quilting section of fabric stores often comes in a wide variety of colours and patterns and have a predictable thickness when mix-and-matching. These are great starter pieces when you begin your sewing journey. Buying fat quarters can give you a fantastic range of patterns to choose from, and there are thousands of 'fat quarter' patterns designed to use exactly what you have and no more.

Knit fabrics make fantastic clothes, and can be forgiving on inaccurate sewing, but they do shift and stretch a lot when sewing, so accidents can be made more frequently. Match knit fabrics to other knit fabrics of the same stretch when mixing in a garment, and perhaps put these projects off until you've mastered a couple of plain cotton fabrics.

Fancy fabrics like crepe can look gorgeous and be

very tactile, but they can be very difficult to sew with. Check how much they fray, and make sure to double stitch or overlock seams if they look prone to destruction.

Always wash fabrics first before you sew them, as the first wash will give the most shrinkage. If you are embroidering a fabric, wash it before you start any embroidery, as shrinkage could distort your stitches. Iron your fabric before laying patterns down and keep your iron handy to tidy up seams as you go.

With embroidery and AIDA cloth, the difference is a little more subtle than with embroidery floss. AIDA cloth is measured by how many threads there are per inch, so you can buy 14ct AIDA cloth from any brand with fair expectation that you will be getting the correct fabric. The texture can vary, however, and I have not managed to find another brand that matches the softness of Zweigart AIDA cloth. I do purchase budget bulk AIDA cloth to test patterns I am designing or use for large projects like cushion covers, but for anything I want to have a finer finish or to be particularly tactile, I buy quality.

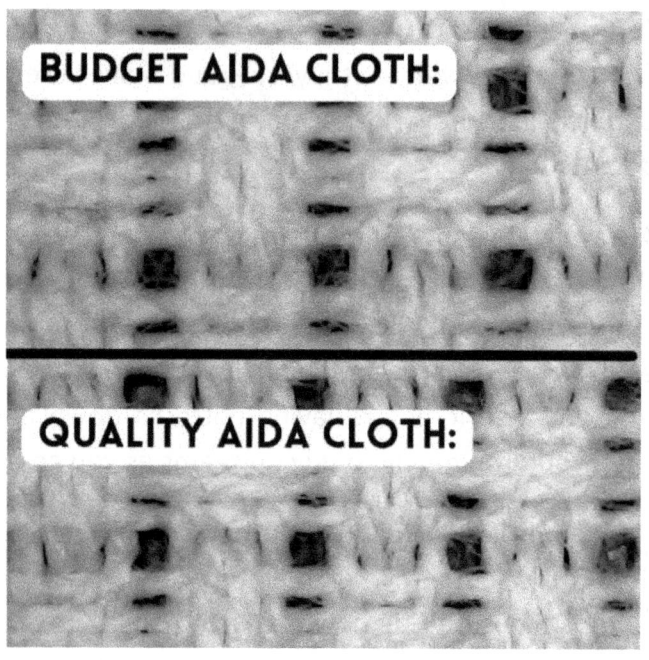

When cutting your patterns, always make sure you have plenty of seam allowance and check what the fraying is like on a test piece of fabric. Some fabrics will fray very easily, and you will find you have less seam allowance than you had when you started especially if the garment has taken a long time to construct and has needed a lot of handling. Some fabrics, such as cotton, respond very well to pinking shears, which cut a zigzag line along your fabric, as you can see in the image.

Pinking shears can reduce the bulk in seams, finish

seams without an overlocker, and generally reduce fraying, but they work best on tightly woven fabrics and items that will not be washed often. They are a great addition to your craft cupboard but are another thing that is worth getting quality as they are very tricky to sharpen.

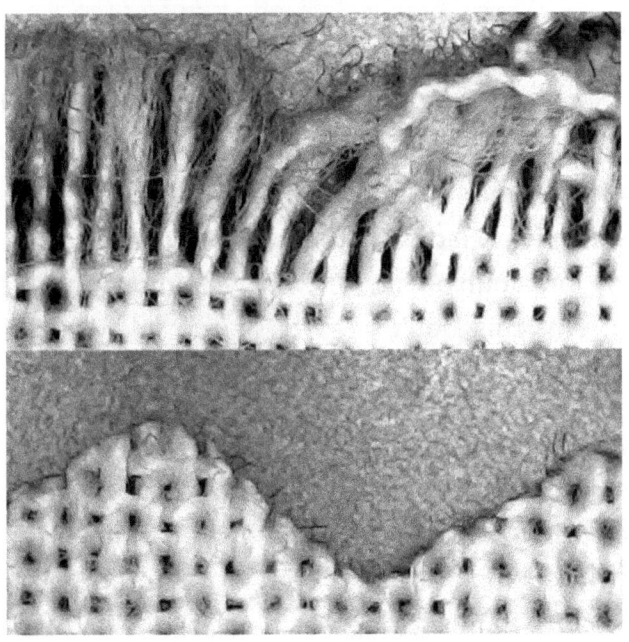

Guide to knitting and crocheting:

Wool comes in different sizes and fibers. The size of the wool will be reflected in the size of needle you will need to work it. Patterns will recommend both the size (ply) of the wool and the size of the needle.

Size 7 to 8mm needles is about average, while a 5.5 or 6mm needle will give you a tighter weave. Chunky wool for large projects like blankets may require larger needles.

Plying is the process of twisting threads together – so 4 ply yarn will consist of 4 threads, and 8 ply yarn will consist of 8 threads.

4 ply yarn is often used for making socks. Baby clothes could range from 2 to 8 ply, but patterns will most commonly ask for 4 or 6 ply yarn. 2 ply wool is used in fancy lacework that requires fine detailing. 8 ply, or double-knit, is very common for craft patterns that don't need to be too fiddly and is a great way to begin.

Wool will also come in different kinds of fibers – acrylic being a synthetic fiber that is cheap and accessible; cotton, being a natural fiber that is often favoured for dishcloths due to its durability; and animal wool which could come from a sheep, an alpaca, a possum or another animal. Some types of wool may shed a lot or be unstable on its own so may be blended with another wool in order to make it easier to use or to make it affordable if one of the materials is more expensive than the one bulking it out. Natural wool fibers are more breathable and help a body to regulate temperature better, so are more effective than acrylic for garments meant to keep a person warm. Baby garments in particular are recommended to be made with natural wool fibers, as since they cannot take a jumper on and off themselves, it keeps them at a more moderate temperature whereas acrylic may cause a baby to overheat.

If you have picked up your wool second hand, you can check what kind it is by using a lighter to conduct the burn test – synthetic fibers will melt, whereas natural fibers will burn naturally.

When starting out knitting, 8ply craft wool and 7 or 8mm needles will be a good way to get a foot in the door on an easy project.

Similarly, with crochet hooks the thicker the yarn the larger the size needle. Yarn manufacturers will give a recommendation for hook size on the label of their wool. When starting out, use a crochet hook that is large enough you can easily see the stitches you are making. Hooks often come in sets, so try some practice stitches and find an easy pattern to go with the size hook you are most comfortable using.

Whether knitting or crocheting, your tension is important – if your tension is too tight or too loose, your measurements may become distorted even if you have counted your stitches correctly. If you stitch a test square, you can measure how many stitches you have per centimeter or inch and you will know whether you will need to adjust your tension, pattern or needle size. It may take a while for your confidence to build up and your tension to become stable, so beginning on simple projects like dishcloths and scarves are a great way to learn the craft before making mistakes using more expensive wool or larger projects which might be discouraging.

Types of needlecrafts:

Cross Stitch:

A common introductory form of embroidery, cross stitch is usually done with embroidery thread such as DMC floss and involves stitching X shaped stitches onto AIDA cloth following a counted pattern. You can find many patterns online or make your own either using grid paper or a computer program. WinStitch is a popular piece of software but does come at a cost. FlossCross is a free pattern maker which operates in the browser but has limitations as you can only store three active patterns at a time.

Colours are not always accurately portrayed on these programs, and can be distorted again by your screen display, so it pays to have physical threads in front of you if in doubt.

To get started on cross stitch, you will need a needle, AIDA cloth, a pattern and some threads and a sharp pair of scissors. Embroidery scissors are very sharp and have very fine blades to make close and accurate cuts. You can get AIDA cloth cut to measure, or in specialty formats like bookmark ribbon.

A thimble and hoop can be beneficial additions to your kit. Thimbles assist in pushing the needle through, which can be a great help especially if you are using a fine AIDA cloth like 18 count or are doing a busy design with top stitching. Using an embroidery hoop assists with keeping the fabric taut and the tension of your stitches even. If your stitches are uneven, it can cause extra puckering and wrinkles in the fabric.

When you begin your project, especially if it is not already organized for you in a kitset, you will want to organize your threads on a card like this with each colour labelled. If your design has similar shades, it can get very easy to mix them up, especially in unnatural or imperfect lighting. Pre-cutting your threads to length can also make the process a lot easier.

DMC thread colours can be identified by the numbers on the band of the thread. There is a master chart which can be bought as a physical copy or found online. Each shade should be specified in your pattern. While other brands, such as Anchor and Semco are also available, DMC is the one I have come across and used the most often and I have found they are very reliable.

DMC threads come in cotton and satin, with six-stranded thread being used in most cross stitch. These threads come in skeins, as pictured, or in cones for those who use them in bulk. Satin threads have a shiny sheen to them, and are usually more expensive, whereas regular cotton threads have a more matte finish.

There are also variegated threads and metallic threads which are more difficult to work with, so I would recommend saving experimenting with those until after you have become acquainted with the basics and have finished some small projects. You can also find glow-in-the-dark thread, small batch dyed threads, and different coloured AIDA fabric once you start branching out, but for now we'll stick to the basics.

When starting out the sheer number of colours can be a bit overwhelming and confusing, but there is a method to the madness. As mentioned earlier, the DMC number on the skein label identifies which colour the thread is. In the DMC chart, colours are organized by both shade and hue. In a shop, you will probably find threads organized by numerical order whereas the chart groups them by colour and type. If you are choosing threads without a specific pattern dictating your colours, or just building your starter's stash, you will want to get a few shades of each of your preferred hues rather than mixing too many different kinds of orange or purple.

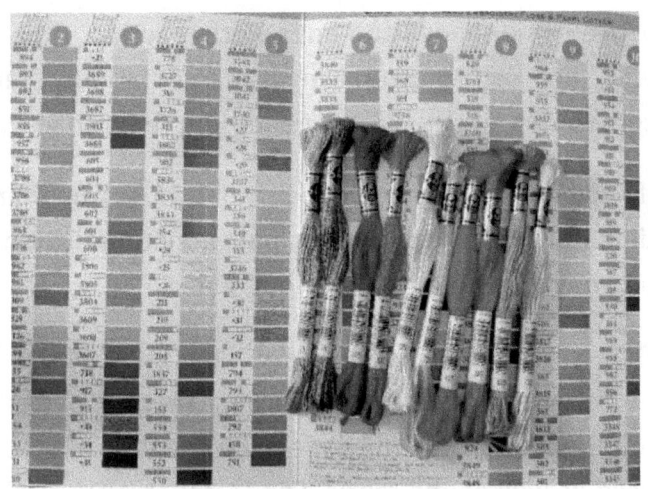

For example, DMC 30 to 32 are different shades of one hue:

DMC 30 – Blueberry Medium Light

DMC 31 - Blueberry

DMC 32 - Blueberry Dark

DMC 208 to 211 are another set of purples:

DMC 208 – Lavender Very Dark

DMC 209 – Lavender Dark

DMC 210 – Lavender Medium

DMC 211 – Lavender Light

While some shades and hues work together, others will not and eye-balling guesstimations can sometimes end up clashing once you're finished.

If you're putting your own patterns together, definitely try to pick your colours in natural lighting and pay attention to the colour codes.

Once your thread is cut to length, the six strands will be separated and used according to your pattern requirements. This will depend on the type of stitch used as well as the fabric. For 14 count AIDA cloth, most patterns I have come across recommend using two strands at a time. This reduces the amount of white fabric that will be visible behind the stitches. Some people may prefer to use three strands for an even 'fuller' look, but the more strands you use the more difficult it can be to pull your needle through, especially if you also have back stitch outlines as many of the designs pictured in this book have.

I would recommend starting out on small patterns while figuring out your preference as everyone stitches slightly differently.

Many beginners get tempted to reduce the number of knots they have to make by using very long lengths of thread. Unfortunately, this often leads to more tangles and knots. The ideal length of thread is the measurement between your wrist and elbow. As I also make designs, I cut my threads to 32cm each time to help me keep track of quantities of threads used in each pattern.

This is what a cross-stitch pattern will look like in most modern cross stitch books. Using colour block patterns can help keep a visual guide of what you are doing to reduce mistakes, but they do come with limitations. If printing a colour block pattern in black and white (like the print version of this book), it can make it harder to read than using symbols only. Even with digital or colour printed pages, the colours printed are approximate and can sometimes be misleading so it is still important to keep track of the symbol as well as the colour, especially where there is only a shade or two different between threads.

Colour Block Pattern

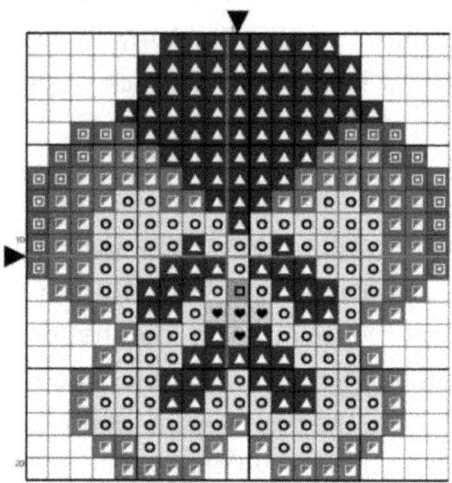

Some patterns will come in black and white symbols only. Some people prefer this if they are printing on a black and white printer or if they are altering colours as they may colour it in by hand with pencils or felts.

Most patterns that are purchased as PDFs online will have options to print both or will specify if they are colour block or symbol only.

Symbol Only Pattern

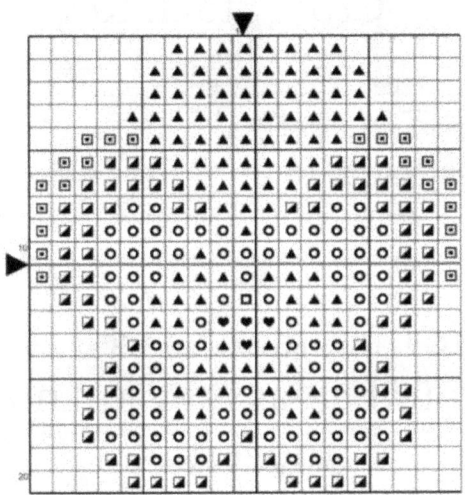

Note the single grey stitch in the middle is a square, whereas the symbols next to it are circles. Mistaking similar symbols is a common mistake, so comparing your pattern to the reference image and marking your pattern before you start is a good idea.

The pattern itself will be accompanied by a key that looks something like this. Keys may include brand and number codes and/or the name of the colour. Sorting your floss and labelling them before you start will help you keep track of them as you go.

Cross Stitch Key

	Number	Name
▫	DMC 648	Beaver Grey light
▲	DMC 550	Violet very dark
▣	DMC 552	Violet medium
◢	DMC 553	Violet
○	DMC 745	Yellow light pale
♥	DMC 743	Yellow medium

Note the brand as well as the number, as they are not universal!

I have included an A4 printable of this pattern on the Bonus Content page of my website at https://laurawolfbookclub.wordpress.com/

To make it easier to keep track of your pattern on larger projects and pick up any mistakes early, you can put basting stitches into your design every ten rows and/or columns. These get pulled out as you reach them. Some AIDA fabric comes pre-printed with guidelines which can then be washed out once complete.

FRONT: **BACK:**

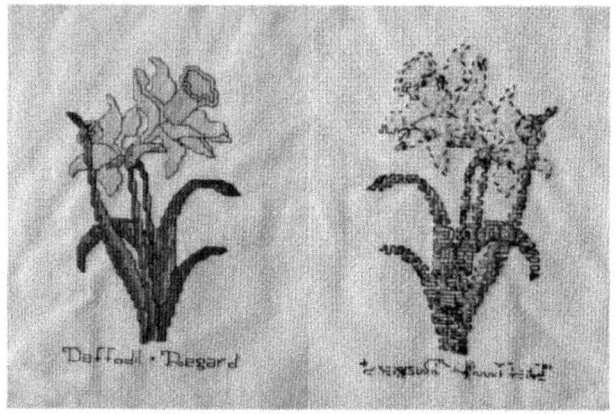

When finished, your cross-stitch design should look something like this. Stopping and starting regularly rather than 'travelling' your thread from section to section keeps the back tidy and less prone to damage.

While the back of your embroidery doesn't necessarily matter if it will be covered and non-visible, having loose 'tails' or stretches of unsecured thread can result in accidental threads being pulled through to the front side as you stitch, and stitches can snag or break if the piece is not finished securely.

These bookmarks, as high-use items, have been finished with calico backing to protect the stitching. For items of clothing, people will sometimes use iron-on backing for protection. For bags or pouches, using the stitched fabric as the outer layer only and having a lining is a good way to keep your stitches safe. For cushion covers, framed pictures or items where the backing is not likely to get rubbed or snagged on anything, the piece might not need anything to protect it at all.

If your item needs to be washed, I recommend only handwashing it and drying it flat to reduce warping the threads. As not all threads are colourfast, it may also be worth making and washing a test swatch to be certain you won't ruin hours of work.

Redwork:

Redwork developed in America in the 19th century and was commonly used on quilts, tablecloths, pillowcases, or basically any blank piece of fabric that could be decorated.

Turkey Red thread was the first colourfast dye readily available to people during this time, which is why it was used on items that would need to be washed frequently. It is done using combinations of basic stitches such as blanket stitch, back stitch, stem stitch, colonial knots etc to make patterns which are first printed or drawn on the fabric using a pencil.

At the turn of the century, preprinted squares of fabric were sold for a penny – called 'penny squares' – which were then stitched and turned into quilts. Some of these designs were given away in subscription magazines, were made by entrepreneurial women as a way to make money from home, or were given as gifts to friends.

The popularity of these penny squares gave redwork a recognizable style which spanned a large geographic area, although there has been a wide range of evolution how redwork has been practiced in years since, and the definition of what exactly redwork is has been stretched beyond embroidery stitches that happen to be red.

By the 1920s different coloured threads were colourfast which led to further evolution of this artform including 'bluework' and multi-coloured redwork. Since blackwork and whitework are their own distinct types of embroidery, and redwork has very distinct characteristics, multicoloured pieces are still often referred to as redwork.

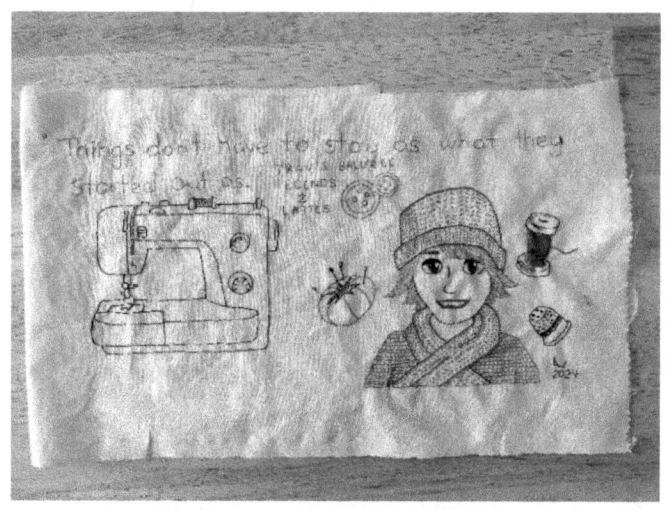

This piece of modern redwork has been made using leftover threads from my cross-stitch kits. The material is plain calico, which is both cheap and a stable evenweave fabric perfect for this type of project.

The images themselves have been printed on paper and then traced onto the fabric using a pencil and lightbox (or awkwardly leaning up against a window).

This character is Emily from Stardew Valley. Emily's jumper has been made with rows of blanket stitch. The outline of her scarf and hat is chain stitch, while the insides are straight zigzags to give the feeling of knitting. Her hair and the straight lines are done using either straight stitch or back stitch. Her eyes are done using satin stitch.

The combination of these stitches creates an impactful mix of textures which creates an engaging and tactile effect.

Blackwork:

Figure 3 'Catherine of Aragon with a Monkey' by Lucas Horenbout, circa 1525-1526.

Blackwork, also known as Spanishwork, was popularized in Europe by Catherine of Aragon who brought the fashion with her. As happens with fashion trends, once Blackwork started to spread it adapted and became its own distinct style that varied from both previous black-on-white embroidery forms found in Britain and Spanish blackwork.

Blackwork is striking and recognizable in many portraits in the 15th and 16th centuries, both as a trim on collars and sleeves and to greater effect in larger garments such as in 'Lady in a Blackwork

Petticoat' by Robert Peake the Elder.

Figure 4 'Lady in a Blackwork Petticoat' by Robert Peake the Elder, circa 1600.

Historic blackwork on garments such as sleeves which need to be visually the same on both sides are worked in 'Holbein stitch', also known as double running stitch or Spanish stitch.

Blackwork is also popular in samplers, cushion covers and in portraits. Blackwork makes use of shading techniques and geometrically planned patterns to create a bold visual effect.

The following is a collection of blackwork stitches

and designs in varying sizes. The complexity of the stitches and the whitespace between them provides a variety of textures.

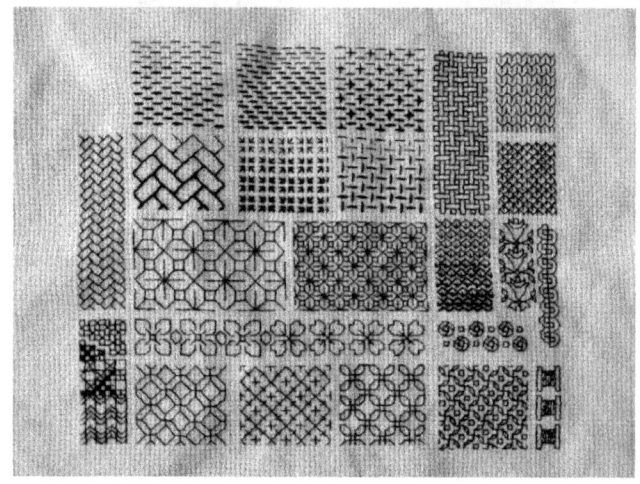

The shading effects in blackwork can be done by controlling how many threads are used. The needle will be threaded with a single thread of floss, and stitches done multiple times to create a transitional effect rather than re-threading a needle with multiple threads each time. Each of the squares below begins with a single stitch at the top of the design through to four stitches at the bottom where the thread is bold and heavy.

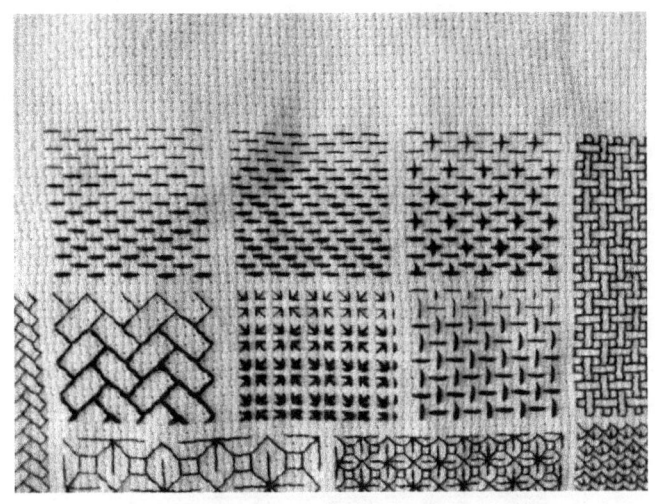

Using this technique, you can achieve interesting effects such as gradients and shadows. It is incredibly affordable to begin, as you will only need to purchase one colour and many patterns are available free online.

Sashiko:

Sashiko is a Japanese traditional mending technique that has become popular all over the world. Sashiko was used by everyday farmers and labourers of the peasant class and so while beautiful, it has practicality at its heart.

Figure 5 Sashiko Jacket, Metropolitan Museum of Art.

Sashiko stitches are designed to provide stability and durability to garments, to patch holes and stabilize fabric before holes form.

Items of clothing would last a long time and become more decorated with age, creating garments that would become valuable heirlooms. Many of these items of clothing would be stitched by more than one person and carry the stories of multiple generations.

Figure 6 Sashiko Stitches, Metropolitan Museum of Art.

Visually, traditional sashiko is often white thread on indigo blue, as that was what material was widely available to the people who used it. Specific patterns would vary from family to family and region to region. Sturdy needles are pushed through multiple stitches at a time using a palm-thimble, creating unique designs that make use of geometry and efficiency.

Modern images online that are labelled 'sashiko' can look very different as people use different materials and diverge from the original tradition, and there is ongoing debate over exactly what sashiko is and where the line lies before it turns into something else. There is also concern that misidentifying contemporary crafts that were inspired by sashiko as still being sashiko is cultural appropriation, as it becomes divorced from its origin.

Sashiko and boro are both textile practices that are deeply rooted in Japanese culture and carry more that can be adequately covered in this brief introduction or by a person such as myself who is not a trained artisan.

There are fantastic resources that have been put together by authentic sashiko artisans such as https://www.japanesesashiko.com/ which can teach you both the technical skills as well as the cultural stories and wisdom that accompany them.

Entry Level Projects:

- Embroidered pockets
- Stitch sampler
- Tote bags for shopping or library trips
- Cushion covers
- Sashiko washcloths

- Knitted or crocheted dishrags
- Granny square blanket
- Knitted or crocheted beanies
- Knitting a straight scarf
- Fabric bookmarks
- Fabric book cover to keep your book safe on the go
- Penny square quilt or potholders
- Picnic basket liner and blanket
- Scrunchies and hair ribbons
- Custom apron
- Scrap fabric coiled basket
- Lavender sachets
- Needle holder book
- Pincushion
- Tablecloth or table runner
- Quilted potholder
- Basic elastic skirt
- Knitted beanie
- Fingerless gloves/sleeves
- Custom pillowcases

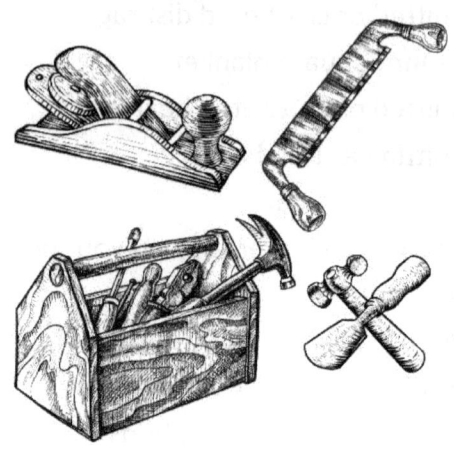

Woodworking

Woodworking comes in many shapes and forms, but working with natural products like wood can be a grounding experience – and one you don't need to invest in power tools to start.

In fact, the lowest bar to entry woodworking is hand carving. You can begin with almost any pocketknife, although carving knives usually have short blades which are easier to control.

There are a few things to keep in mind when picking up carving as a new hobby:

Keep your knife sharp. This will mean you will need

to apply less pressure and will be able to make more accurate cuts – more pressure on a blunt blade is what often causes injuries.

Cut away from you, not towards, and primarily move the wood rather than the blade. This will keep your slips to a minimum.

Stock up on band aids and a good first aid kit, because it's inevitable you will cut yourself.

Freshly cut green wood has more moisture and is easier to cut than dried hard wood. Different varieties of wood are softer or harder than others, so pick an easy soft wood for your early projects.

Straight grains are easier to cut than curly grain, and knots within the wood may complicate your design – look at the wood and work with its natural form. Try to cut with the grain rather than against the grain for clean and smooth cuts.

Not all types of wood are food safe. If you are making something that will be used for food, such as a spoon, spatula, bowl or kuksa – make sure you can identify the wood and be sure it is suitable for its intended use.

Be aware of the hazards with materials you will use

such as linseed oil – which needs to be stored carefully with contaminated rags disposed of with caution as it can combust easily.

If you want to invest in a lathe or other more advanced equipment, see if you can find some mentoring and learn how to use it safely. Find out if there are any woodworking groups in your area, as hands-on experience is the best way to get better at a hobby. Always maintain your machinery carefully, as even a slight misalignment can lead to injury.

Investing in a sharpening system can not only keep your woodworking tools sharp but your kitchen and craft equipment as well. Knowing good sharpening and maintenance processes can also help you save a lot of money as you will be able to restore old tools that might just need some TLC. Sharpening services are also a great side-gig that could subsidize your hobby as well as connecting you to your community.

Please also keep in mind ventilation when working with wood, particularly when using chemicals and sanding. Fine dust from sanding can get into your lungs and create long-term health concerns, so it is worth getting an appropriate grade mask and making sure your ventilation is adequate.

Entry Level Projects:

- Spatula and spoon carving
- Decorative carving – select a piece of firewood and practice shaping it
- Flat chopping boards (end-grain chopping boards can be deceptively hard as the wood will expand and retract, leaving gaps. For a first project a simple, nicely shaped chopping board is perfect)
- Lazy Susan
- Laundry caddy
- Tea tray
- Small bookshelf
- Outdoor chairs
- Raised garden beds
- Birdhouse
- Bug hotel

Photography

The only way to get good at photography is to take photos. Luckily, you don't need a lot of equipment to get started.

You can even take your first steps with your smart phone if an SLR camera is out of your budget range or you're not sure if it is a hobby you'll commit to. Keep an eye out at secondhand stores or online until one within your price range comes along – photography *can* turn into an expensive hobby if you start getting quality lenses, and it can definitely be worth it if it is what you love, but it's worth getting familiar with things before spending up large.

When starting out in photography, spend some time learning how to hold your camera correctly – while often overlooked, this can impact the quality of your pictures as camera shake can cause you to take blurry images. There will be many situations where you will not be using a tripod, so practicing conscientious camera positioning can contribute to your foundational camera skills.

Always use two hands and consider how you are braced for stability. You can crouch down, lean on a wall, or spread your legs in a wider stance for better stability.

Take your time practicing with your settings and learning the theory behind the exposure triangle – the relationship between the three main factors of photography that will give you varying results for the same shot: ISO, aperture, and shutter speed.

ISO controls the light sensitivity of your camera or film. The lower the ISO setting, the less sensitive to light while the higher the ISO the higher the sensitivity. This will change depending on your location and lighting. For example, shooting outdoors may require an ISO setting between 100 to

200 while indoor or night photography might require 400 to 800 or even higher depending on the level of light available. For controlled light environments as you are learning how your camera behaves, you may wish to both alter the ISO and take several shots with the lights on and off, the curtains open and closed, or with additional lamps and reflectors to see how the results vary.

THE EXPOSURE TRIANGLE

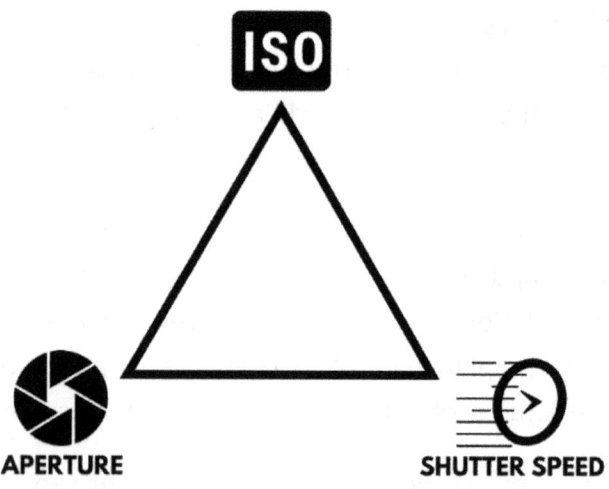

The aperture is the opening of your camera lens, which widens or contracts to alter the amount of light admitted into the camera. The 'f-stop' refers to the ratio of your lens's focal length – a wider aperture will be indicated by a lower f-number and a narrower aperture will be indicated by a larger f-number.

If you wanted to isolate your object, you would use a wide aperture. If you wanted to keep the entire scene in focus, like for photographing groups of people, you would want a narrow aperture.

Shutter speed controls how long the shutter will remain open and also impacts how much light is allowed into your shot. Fast shutter speeds are used for sharp action shots and result in a crisp image, while longer shutter speeds will blur motion. Long exposure shots can be used in night photography to capture streaking lights like stars or cars headlights.

Setting up your subject and your lighting is a huge part of getting the right shot. For portraits, make sure the light is coming from behind you – you may need to adjust your position a few times until you get things just right, especially if it is a sunny day and there are strong shadows. Overcast days make for great photos as the light contrast is less intense. The 'golden hour' is when the light is just right for amazing photos with a warm hue. Golden hour happens twice a day – the first hour after sunrise and the last hour before sunset. Make a habit of taking your camera out during these times and seeing what pictures you can capture.

There are countless books, videos and blogs that can teach you camera skills, but the most important thing is to enjoy the process of discovery.

Consider getting yourself a nice frame to display your favourite print of the month, and an album or scrapbook to log your progression in skill and style.

Photography challenges:

Photograph one object at different angles, from different perspectives and at different depths. Play with the lighting and location of the object and arrange your photos by order of preference.

Choose a colour and search out things to photograph in that colour. How many yellow objects are there in and around your home? Don't dismiss objects like switches or miscellaneous things in your junk drawer.

Take an object like a teacup or a small figurine and take photos of it in different locations.

Stage one area of your house and take photos of it from the same location at different times of day and in different weather. Return to the same location over the course of the year and look at how the room changes.

Go for a walk in a local park and take photos of flowers. Play around with filters on your editing software or apps to see how you can adjust the colours.

Dress up with a friend and have a picnic somewhere scenic. Take photos of each other and try to capture the vibe of the outing, including the weather.

Photograph an item in your home and play with natural and artificial light to see how the look changes. Try moving yourself so the light is behind you, versus in front of you. Try opening and closing the curtains and using lamps. Make note of what you've changed for each shot so when you're comparing them in your editing phase you can isolate what elements you like for your preferred look.

Commonplace Books

Have you ever bought a journal but struggled to know what to put in it? Or perhaps had a change of heart part way through and felt like your next contribution would ruin the theme?

Commonplace books are a type of journal that are seeing a comeback due to their willingness to embrace the chaotic. Rather than adhering to any particular rules or forms like bullet journalling or pre-printed journalling pages, commonplace books serve as a location for anything and everything that inspires you.

Like a quote? Jot it down.

Receive a gift that brought you joy? Keep a piece of the wrapping paper along with a note of what you received and who from.

Come across a recipe you love? Transcribe it for later use.

From pressed flowers to movie stubs to torn pieces of magazines or written memories, this book serves as a common place for it all – get it?

And best of all – you've finally got a place to start using washi tape and stickers!

Whereas journals serve as a record of thoughts or events, commonplace books are generally used as a repository of things that spark inspiration – whether it is for mental health, travel inspiration or creative endeavours. A commonplace book will reflect the interest and personality of the person compiling it.

In the days of Aristotle, Cicero, and Seneca, readers collected 'commonplace ideas' that they found worth collecting, each with their own preferences and values.

Marcus Aurelius' *'Meditations'* was one of these – originally a private collection of his own thoughts and ideas, which is now available in multiple translations and editions.

Leonardo da Vinci also kept a commonplace book called *'The Codex Arundel'* where he recorded his thoughts and diagrams for later use. He described its purpose as "collection without order, drawn from many papers, which I have copied here, hoping to arrange them later each in its place, according to the subjects of which they treat."

Other notable people who have kept commonplace books are:

- Francis Bacon
- Robert Burns
- E. M. Forster
- Thomas Jefferson
- H. P. Lovecraft
- John Milton
- Isaac Newton
- Ronald Reagan
- Virginia Woolf
- And Sherlock Holmes, from Arthur Conan Doyles' literary world

If you have a spare notebook, you can start immediately! Have a think about what you might like to collect and look around your home to see if there is anything you would like to include to begin your journey.

Ideas to get you started:

- A list of your favourite books in your library, or from your wishlist
- Favourite quotes or song lyrics
- Pressed flowers
- Samples of fabric
- Cut out pictures from magazines
- Newspaper articles
- Written records of favourite memories
- New recipes
- Tried and tested favourite recipes
- Travel destinations
- Sketches

Don't overthink it! Just capture anything that keeps your attention.

Paper crafts

Paper crafts have the wonderful benefit of being extremely affordable and accessible. Different types of paper crafts suit different people as some demand precision and perfection of technique whereas others are freer for adaptation and imperfection. They all provide a slow and meditative hobby that provides tactile, visual and mental stimulation which can help your overall wellbeing.

Origami

Origami is associated with the traditional Japanese art, but the definition has expanded to include all kinds of paper folding including gift wrapping.

The benefits of origami have been measured in school aged children and have found to assist with several different areas of development including mathematics, handwriting and special awareness.[7] Origami has also become popular amongst seniors as a mode of creative expression and cognitive exercise.

Origami has endless possibilities as you can learn from others designs or create your own. I had a friend at university who was so talented at origami that when I dared him to make a double headed dragon, he quickly adapted a simple paper crane design and produced one within about a minute.

Paper cranes are very popular and are an excellent way to learn origami. In Japanese folklore, the crane (or *tsuru*) symbolizes honour, good fortune, loyalty and longevity. There is a myth that it lives for a thousand years, and if you fold one thousand paper

---

[7] Travers BG, Kirkorian HL, Jiang MJ, et al. *Knowing How to Fold 'em: Paper Folding across Early Childhood*, 2018.

cranes you will be given good fortune and granted a wish.

Figure 7 Statue of Sadako Sasaki with a Paper Crane by Hazel Reeves

Sadako Sasaki spread the popularity of making a thousand cranes across the globe as people heard her story. Born in 1943, she was two years old when she was exposed to radiation during the bombing of Hiroshima. After being diagnosed with leukemia ten years later, she set out to make 1000 paper cranes during her stay in hospital. A novel by Eleanor Coerr, *Sadako and the Thousand Paper Cranes*, is based off her story although in the novel she never completed her goal with her friends coming through for her after her death. The real-life Sadako is said to have exceeded her goal during her lifetime, with her classmates sparking a movement commemorating the loss of Sadako and other victims of the bomb which resulted in a worldwide movement for peace and the erection of the Children's Peace Monument as well as several other sculptures inspired by her memory.

Paper cranes have now become a recognizable symbol of peace as well as general well-wishes. A wreath of a thousand paper cranes is a common gift to a loved friend or family member suffering an illness or injury, often being made by a community of people coming together to wish them recovery.

Making 1001 cranes is also a popular wedding tradition, with 1000 cranes being made by the bride and wedding party and another bonus crane being made by the groom for extra luck.

Figure 8 A paper crane curtain from my wedding.

Paper cranes are very versatile, as they can be laid flat and posted with letters, stacked and strung into wreaths or hung into curtains. The look can change drastically by using white, coloured or patterned paper.

Figure 9 An origami bridal bouquet from my wedding.

Origami can make fantastic decoration and décor as well as practical items. When I got married, we were fairly young and poor having just been students and having completed a year as a nanny – a very low-paid job I took with adventure in mind rather than profit! We had an origami theme which was important to me as I'd been making paper cranes for years. For months leading up to the wedding, friends and family folded cranes, and I made origami flowers for a bouquet with my fiancé's younger sisters out of patterned scrapbooking paper. The result was gorgeous, and they have been a lasting reminder of all of the personal love and time invested into our lives by all of those people.

Origami can also make lovely gifts and activities to do with children – you can make interactive toys like jumping frogs, flapping butterflies, or even ninja stars.

Paper Quilling

Like origami, you can buy pre-cut paper intended for quilling in regular width strips, or you can make your own. It definitely will make your life easier to get pre-cut strips and good quality glue though, as you may end up using a lot of them.

Paper quilling can be an art that follows a plan, or something more organic as you play with different colours, shapes and widths. You can glue your paper onto cards or framed artwork for the wall. The main techniques to master are how to make the core shapes using coils, scrolls and sharp folds.

Your main tools will be a quilling tool, a pair of sharp scissors and a quilling comb – which while optional, is very handy in making a great variety of shapes that could be very fiddly and difficult to manage without it. A quilling board can also be very useful – these are foam or cork boards with uniform holes that can help you make your shapes with precision.

Tips to get started:

Dedicate a space and keep it organized and clean.

Start simple – small, completed designs will help you build the skills necessary to take on bigger and more complicated projects.

Practice consistently in small chunks of time and take breaks – fatigue will be the greatest contributor to mistakes and frustration.

Use quality paper cut to uniform widths and quality glue that fits the purpose.

Learn a bit about colour theory, stay open-minded and experiment. Playing around will help you find your own personal artistic flavour.

Look after your supplies – keep your supplies in containers to keep them dust-free and consider either sealing your work with a topcoat spray or having it mounted in a display case to keep it from damage, dirtiness or decay.

Drawing and Painting

Anyone can draw – and drawing well is really all a matter of perspective and opinion. The *hardest* thing, I think, is trying to get exactly what you are imagining in your brain to come out through your hands – and that is a feat even some of the greatest painters struggled with.

Vincent van Gogh painted over canvases several times, and Monet famously took a knife to several of his works out of anger and dissatisfaction.

The lesson to take from this is that there really is no

lid on mastery – but that doesn't mean the process of trying is completely worthless. Even those destroyed works of Monet's would be a lot finer than anything I could manage to paint – and I would have loved to see van Gogh's rejected works, even if he did not think them worth preserving.

Don't be afraid to start, and don't be afraid to make mistakes. If you do a little drawing regularly, it may be wonderful to be able to look back on the journey of how far you've come. Consider getting yourself a small sketchbook and pencil to take out with you on walks and make a habit of drawing trees or small blooms in quiet moments.

There are plenty of artists who have put together little art kits that fit inside Altoids mint containers for taking on the go – cutting pencils and paper small enough, or even setting up a basic palette of paints.

Watercolour can be another avenue, or even using herbal teas to paint on watercolour paper. Find colours that resonate with you and look to your environment for inspiration. What would you like to take a moment to appreciate? Is there anything you would like to introduce?

Getting yourself a frame or easel for the size of your

pad could provide another opportunity to display your favourite pictures, as you can layer your favourite one on the top and adjust them as often as you want. You could have sketches that fit each season, based off the flowers in your garden or images you find important or symbolic to you, or just display your best sketch of the week.

Copying others work is also a valid way to learn a style – while I do not support plagiarism or making money from copying other's work exactly, finding pictures you like and trying to emulate their styles is something artists have been doing for about as long as art has existed.

Eventually, through trial and error, you will discover what you are capable of and which styles you prefer – and as you grow in skill you can develop a style of your own.

Upcycling

Upcycling and restoring used goods can be so therapeutic and enjoyable and is a great expression of cottagecore values. As mentioned earlier, with the rise of 'planned obsolescence' a lot of products made to modern standards and expectations are not very durable, so *finding* old things that were made well and keeping them in good condition, or extending the life of products through modification or restoration is both satisfying as well as an expression of living out of a set of values that have been condemned by guys wearing ties like Mr. Bernard London.

One necessary word of warning is to consider the source and nature of the objects you are using and whether or not they could pose a health risk for the purpose you would like to use it for. Modern health and safety standards are a lot higher than they used to be, and second-hand goods from unknown sources may not meet the recommended standards.

Old teacups, dishware and other crockery, for example, may have high levels of toxic metals like lead and cadmium. Lead and cadmium have been linked to development of cancer and adverse effects on the immune system.[8] Long term exposure to toxic metals can cause chronic health issues, and for children there is no safe limit for exposure as it has been known to affect cognitive and behavioural development.[9]

Heavy metals are often used in paints, dyes and glazes, so colourful crockery – particularly the kinds that have pictures on the inside where you eat or drink out of, or colours near the rim – can be particularly risky. The safest choices are plain dishware with uncoloured glazes, or glassware. Some crockery will also use toxic metals but seal them beneath a non-toxic glaze – so damaged or chipped tableware should be treated with caution.

---

[8] https://www.ncbi.nlm.nih.gov/pmc/articles/PMC7203386/
[9] https://ceh.org/yourhealth/lead-in-dishes/

If you know the original brand, you may be able to contact the company and ask whether their products contain heavy metals and in what quantities, or if it is a favourite object you could get a lead testing kit from a hardware store. There are some lead awareness groups that will take equipment around the community and host testing days, so it may be worth looking into if there is anyone in your area.

Old teacups that are not safe to drink from can be turned into other artistic objects like candles, bird feeders or pot plant pots for shallow rooted plants like succulents. Creative thinking and an afternoon spent on Pinterest can help you come up with ideas on how to do just about anything.

Also be aware of possible toxicity before using reclaimed timber. Old floorboards and the like from demolition projects can be a fantastic source of cheap and characterful wood, but if the type of wood is not food-safe, it has been treated or it has been contaminated with lead nails, it isn't a good choice for projects like chopping boards that are intended for food use.

Likewise, wood that was intended for outside use is often treated and not food safe.

Check in at your local thrift stores and online sales platforms regularly for bargains and remember that it may take a few experimental projects to develop a skill. Make sure you have a well-ventilated area and appropriate safety gear (such as a respiratory mask or gloves) before getting too carried away.

Old broken items can be deconstructed, and the components saved for future projects. Fabric can be cut down into easily stored rectangles and components like buckles, buttons, D-Rings, or odds and ends like furniture handles can be stored in tackle boxes until needed.

Things to include in your upcycling toolkit:

- Screwdrivers
- Sandpaper
- All-purpose wood varnish
- Card scraper
- Utility knife
- Sticker-removal solution
- Hot glue gun
- Epoxy
- Disposable gloves
- Respiratory mask
- Paint

- Power drill
- Scissors for dedicated purposes (fabric, paper, messy objects)
- Sewing kit
- Misc tools (pliers, hammer, Allen keys etc)
- Measuring tape, level and rulers
- WD-40

Some great entry level projects are:

- Restoring old furniture with sanding and varnish or paint. Switch up the handles for a fresh look.
- Cut and sew old t-shirts into shopping bags.
- Wind and hot glue macrame cord around objects like glass bottles and tissue boxes to provide matching natural tone décor.
- Melt beeswax onto plain cotton squares to make eco-friendly sandwich wraps. Make sure to use a dedicated pan, as once waxy it will be difficult to clean.
- Rehandle thrifted knives and sharpen them up like new.
- Give old books new life by making them new covers – there are plenty of tutorials on bookbinding across the internet.
- Use scrap craft and wrapping paper to make

bookmarks.
- Cut the pictures out of old cards and use them to make new ones.
- Find old and unloved embroidery projects at the op shop and turn them into bags.
- Find obsolete objects (like cassette tapes) and decorate them to make themed Christmas tree decorations.
- Use printable templates to create your own decorative storage boxes.
- Thrift old photo frames and find interesting things to put in them. A fabric backing with ribbons can become a useful place to keep hair clips.

Poetry

Ah, what shall I be at fifty
Should Nature keep me alive,
If I find the world so bitter
When I am but twenty-five?
- Alfred Tennyson, Maud

Poetry is a fantastic way to practice capturing emotions and expressing your thoughts. By the nature of slowing down and ruminating on which words to use and how to frame your thoughts, you learn to hold each moment in the palm of your hands and appreciate them in new ways.

There are so many forms of poetry to explore, from structured verse to freeform poetry which tends to be raw and honest, not relying on consistent rhymes or meter. Each type of poem has different characteristics, so exploring them to find which resonate with you is a great idea.

Keeping a blank notebook of poetry to copy down poems you come across that speak to you is a great practice to nourish a literary soul. To get you started, we'll go over the basics of two types of poetry that resonate with cottagecore values. From here, you can play around and build your own preferences.

Free verse is another type of poetry that is as flexible as thought itself and is very popular with contemporary poets due to its freedom of expression. Like art, it can consist of utterly anything as you put pen to paper, so don't be afraid of starting.

Idylls

An idyll is a simple poem that celebrates rural and country lifestyles, emerging from Greek and Roman poets following the tradition of Theocritus. Many later poets followed a chain of inspiration that points back towards Theocritus' vision of Arcadia as was covered in the first chapter of this book, although each poet has put their own shifting values into its changing form. They often focus on farmers or labourers and daily rustic tasks, or of laying down to rest in the scenic countryside surrounded by nature and sometimes fae-folk creatures including nymphs and sartyrs.

O, for a lodge in some vast wilderness,
Some boundless contiguity of shade!
- William Cowper, The Task

I SUFFER, heart and brain,
In weariness and pain;
My soul faints, and I tire
Of all the sordid strife,
Day after day, in which I waste my life –
Toiling for nothing higher
Than that vile gold, for want of which the poor
Must give to carking cares
Youth, manhood, and gray hairs,
To scare the wolves of famine from the door.
I've sought the sylvan solitudes,
Where, far apart from all the noise of men,
Amid romantic woods
Streams wander through soft sunlight and sweet gloom,
Down the green hill and through the rocky glen;
And where the fair flowers bloom,

And happy birds sing to the capering leaves
A song that never tires and never grieves.
And there, (as in the days
Of careless boyhood,) I will sit and gaze
Around in idle freedom, with my head
Against the trunk of some gnarled oak wide-spread;
And there I'll hear the birds exalt their mirth
In music born alike of heaven and earth,
While graceful shadows in their hammocks swing,
Like gentle woodnymphs, where the wild flowers spring:
And there I'll watch the clouds
Drifting in stately crowds,
Like stately ships with banners streaming high,
Across the trackless ocean of the sky;
And blissful castles shall my fancies build
In those blue fields by mortal plows untilled;
While on the wave-like music of the birds
Shall drift my dreams too fair for mortal words:
And thus shall I forget
The present with its Gorgons of regret,
Its Satyr-like ambitions and despairs,
And all its Vulcan brood of limping cares!
- Clarence A Buskirk, *A Cavern for a Hermitage*

Idylls have been a source of cottagecore expression and inspiration all through history, through a mixture of hindsight and appreciation of the present. Alfred Tennyson published *'Idylls of the King'* between 1859 to 1885 in a series of twelve poems reimagining the legends around King Arthur, whereas Henry David Thoreau's poetry has been described as an American Idyll and was written largely from his perspective of his present moment. Much of Thoreau's work, including the bulk of the content of his masterpiece *Walden*, was written during the period of time he lived alone in a log cabin in the woods.

"I went to the woods because I wished to live deliberately, to front only the essential facts of life, and see if I could not learn what it had to teach, and not, when I came to die, discover that I had not lived. I did not wish to live what was not life, living is so dear; nor did I wish to practise resignation, unless it was quite necessary. I wanted to live deep and suck out all the marrow of life..."
-David Henry Thoreau, *Walden (excerpt)*

Poetry then, does not need to be always looking back in hindsight to be considered an idyll. Some, like Theocritus and Tennyson look to the past for an out-of-reach ideal, while others like Cowper and Thoreau capture their present state of being in order to process their experiences and desires and live their lives with intentionality. Idylls are better defined by their content and their message than by any specific style guides.

Figure 10 Portrait of Matsuo Bashō by Hokusai, late 18th century.

Haiku

Haiku are poems of Japanese origin that date back to the 17th Century, although earlier forms existed as early as the 13th Century. They are unrhymed form consisting of 17 syllables in three lines – 5 in the first, 7 in the second and 5 in the third line. Early haiku dealt primarily with descriptions of nature and seasons designed to evoke an emotional response.

The great poet Matsuo Bashō of the Tokugawa Period put his own spin on the form, and his influence spread across Japan.

'The Old Pond' by Matsuo Bashō is arguably the most famous haiku. It has various English translations which evoke different imagery, but the literal translation reads like this:
Fu-ru (old) i-ke (pond) ya,
ka-wa-zu (frog) to-bi-ko-mu (jumping into)
mi-zu (water) no o-to (sound)

Translation by Fumiko Saisho:
The old pond-
a frog jumps in,
sound of water.

Translation by Alan Watts:
The old pond,
A frog jumps in:
Plop!

I've seen this poem also titled 'Ancient Pond', which evokes a slightly different picture. When you break down ideas into this minimalist form, each word can alter the image into something quite different, and English as a hybrid language is incredibly diverse to work with.

Haiku often introduce one idea in the first line, another in the second and the third line gives the spark of relationship between them. The frog in this poem may seem energetic, curious, natural, or disturbing depending on the words and preferred arrangement of the imagery. Some translations aim to appreciate the meditative quality of the image, others approach the idea with more levity or irreverence.

Sengai Gibon, one of Bashō's disciples penned a parody of The Old Pond featuring his master:

The old pond!
Bashō jumps in,
the sound of water.

Another poem by Bashō captures a gritty picture of the hardships of his travels:

Fleas, lice
horse pissing
by the pillow.

Other poets such as Yosa Buson, Kobayashi Issa, Masaoka Shiki, Takahama Kyoshi and Kawahigashi Hekigotō continued the adaptation and spread of haiku throughout the ages and into the 20th Century.

Haiku continued to develop and spread internationally at an incredible rate after World War II, and today people practice it in many different styles all over the world.

My personal favourite haiku was written by Kobayashi Issa shortly after the loss of one of his children:

The world of dew,
is a world of dew,
and yet, and yet.

It speaks to me on a deep level of yearning, mourning, love and pain that evokes a much bigger image than the simplicity of the individual words.

Hattori Ransetsu, another of Bashō's students, also penned a heavy hitting haiku which paints a vivid picture of a woman he came across in his travels:

The childless woman,
how tenderly she caresses
homeless dolls...

Each of these images paints a very clear picture which develops further with every line. While the words are minimalist, the images are vivid, thought provoking and profound.

Another of Kobayashi Issa's haiku, 'O Snail' resonates with my slow living ethos and cottagecore lifestyle, particularly since I live with a chronic illness and use pacing as an integral part of life.

O snail,
Climb Mount Fuji,
But slowly, slowly!

What a beautiful picture of a small humble and fragile creature accomplishing a great feat with slow perseverance and fortitude.

In the 2016 movie *Hunt for the Wilderpeople*, directed by Taika Waititi, the main characters use haiku to connect with each other. Delinquent Ricky Baker explains he has been taught to compose them by his social worker to help him express his feelings and uses them throughout the movie to shocking and sometimes hilarious effect. By the end of the movie, Uncle Hec calls out to Ricky and expresses himself in a haiku as well, while counting the syllables on his fingers:

Me and this fat kid,
We ran and we ate and read books,
And it was the best.
-Hec, Hunt for the Wilderpeople

Haiku are a wonderful form of poetry to play with as it has minimal restrictions, making the possibilities infinite. It's extremely short form also allows you to home in on one subject in order to spark an emotional reaction from a single granular concept.

Practice is the best way to improve, and even if you find it difficult to start, as you proceed down your haiku journey you will grow your vocabulary and instinct on how to string words together.

To finish this segment, I leave you with a final haiku on the process of writing by Katsushika Hokusai:

I write, erase, rewrite
Erase again, and then,
A poppy blooms.

Wholesome Cooking

The kitchen is the centre of the cottagecore home, and for a very good reason. Food feeds not only the stomach, but your entire wellbeing. Why else would people comfort-eat?

Memories that use more than one sense stick in our mind a lot longer than experiences that primarily are focused on just one. Scents and tastes come with powerful imagery and feelings – if you've seen the movie Ratatouille, that scene where the food critic is blown back to his childhood comes to mind.

Do you have any foods that remind you of your childhood, or people you care about? Do you have a cookbook that you've inherited? Cooking those dishes can bring you closer to those people, even if they have passed away.

Occasionally in the autumn, I'll make pumpkin soup with cumin and a generous topping of grated cheese. It was my father's favourite soup, and despite the fact he died when I was very young, and I have no actual memories of *him* eating the soup. It still feeds an emotional part of me that wants to nurture and enjoy that connection. We are separated by decades as well as the very real line of life and death, but we are eating and enjoying the same soup.

Ginger Crunch reminds me of my mother, but I find it too sweet and sugary to indulge in often, so it's something I would prefer just a taste of and to give the rest to someone else. A great recipe for a shared lunch!

Russian fudge reminds me of my grandmother, and the times when I made it with her and sold it on a roadside stall outside her house.

Simple scones, and particularly ones with jam and fresh whipped cream remind me of all the wonderful times I had at the church I grew up in, or the special times we would make it for events like Mother's Day.

Porridge with a healthy dose of honey or brown sugar still reminds me of the morning breakfasts around the table we would have when we stayed with my grandparents.

Fresh honeycomb reminds me of visiting my great uncle who had a hive in his garden and the amazing honey on fresh bread I had at his house.

What dishes do you have that have importance to you? Close your eyes and think back to any moments around food. Focus on the flavours and on the emotions that accompany them. Make a list of those foods and make an effort to hunt down the recipes, so you have them on hand whenever you want to re-spark those good vibes.

The act of cooking can be very therapeutic, especially if you've become a person who relies on convenience food. Using whole ingredients, spices and herbs rather than premade sauces also gives you a great sense of control over the flavour and you can create your own signature dishes that perhaps one day people will remember nostalgically when they think about you!

Make a list of the foods you love and organize your pantry accordingly, so you've always got the staples on hand. Using seasonal fruits and vegetables is also really important – not only for feeling connected to the seasons, but for keeping your food budget reasonable!

I recommend trying out using rough ingredients like stoneground flour at least once as well – it creates a much denser finished product, but the flavour and character of it is amazing.

Also look into the items you use in the kitchen. If you'll be using them a lot, having nice equipment can make everything a lot more enjoyable.

Be wary of retro plastic baking containers though, as the ones made pre-60s in particular may contain chemicals that aren't food safe.

I prefer using clear containers so you can see the baking inside, as the way your food is displayed provides additional enjoyment.

Some recipes to get you started:

Fancy Porridge

Porridge is a simple staple that has been enjoyed for centuries – and for good reason. It gives you a slow-burning energy that can last well beyond lunchtime.

It can be made either with water or milk for a creamier texture. But in the modern age, we've got so many more options to jazz up the flavour. Try experimenting with different options until you find something you love!

Base recipe:
½ cup rolled oats
1 to 1 ½ cups water or milk

Mix in a saucepan and heat on a moderate heat stove until thick and creamy.

Extra additions:
Chia seeds
Cinnamon
Seeds or nuts
Berries
Dried fruit
Chocolate chips or cocoa/cacao
Peanut butter or tahini
Stone fruit (peaches, plums, cherries)
Cooked apple
Sliced banana
Greek yoghurt
Nutritional powders

Scones

The perfect morning or afternoon snack, and so easy to whip up for friends coming around! You can add ham, cheese, curry powder and turmeric for a savoury edition, or chopped dates to sweeten them – or the traditional jam and cream (or cream and jam depending on your preference).

Base recipe:
3 cups self-raising flour (or add 6 tsp baking powder to plain flour)
Pinch of salt
75g softened butter
1 to 1 ½ cups milk
Extra flour for kneading
Extra milk for glaze

Rub softened butter into flour and salt until it resembles breadcrumbs – or alternatively, mix with a knife.
Mix in milk until combined.
Toss onto a floured board and knead lastly until smooth.
Cut and place on lined oven tray at least 2cm apart, brush tops with extra milk.
Bake at 220C/420F for 12 minutes until tops are slightly golden.

For pinwheel scones, roll into a flat rectangle with a floured rolling pin. Spread with butter, then add filling and roll up into a log. Cut carefully with a floured knife into 1-inch discs.

For clotted cream, add a small handful sugar to cream and whip with a hand mixer until it peaks.

Decorative Quiche

You can't get much more cottagecore than wholesome eggs. You also don't have to look far on Pinterest before you find amazing quiches decorated with vegetables and flowers. Quiche can be as joyful and colourful as you want it to be, and it's a great way to make a gorgeous-but-edible table centerpiece.

Use this base recipe and whatever veggies or edible flowers you have on hand.

Base recipe:
Crust:
1 cup flour
½ tsp salt
¼ cup olive oil or bran oil
¼ cup refrigerated water

Mix well and press into a greased oven dish. Double

or triple recipe for large dishes.

Quiche:
Eggs
Milk
Grated cheese
Additional veggies

Crack as many eggs as you need to completely cover the bottom of your dish.
Pour in a little milk until it clouds around the yolks.
Mix together lightly with a fork.
Add in grated cheese (12 cup to 1 cup or so depending on the size of your dish) until the quiche filling feels stable enough to support the vegetables.
Slice vegetables and arrange on the top of your quiche. Start with the largest pieces (ie: tomato slices) and add in smaller pieces to fill the gaps.
Bake at 200C/400F for approximately 30 minutes. You can check your quiche is done by inserting a knife into it and checking it is clear when removed.

Basic Bread

People have been making bread since the Neolithic age. Bread has been made all over the world in a lot of different ways – which means it is pretty hard to get wrong.

If you haven't made bread before, you'll find that the flavour and texture can change quite drastically depending on which ingredients you use and how you prepare your dough. There are endless recipes to try, but I recommend you try altering a few things yourself – add a little oil, switch out some water for milk, change up your kneading technique or incorporate some extra ingredients like spices or herbs and find out what you like. Eventually, you'll pick up on what it is you like in a loaf and you'll have your own recipe that is tailored to your tastes. Try out this base recipe and mix and match it with some of the alterations below:

1 ½ cup lukewarm water
1 Tbsp dry yeast
4 cups flour
1 pinch salt

Sprinkle yeast over lukewarm water and leave for 10 mins to activate until frothy.

Mix yeast-water mixture with dry ingredients and knead lightly on a flour-covered board into a doughy ball.

Place the dough into a greased bowl and cover with plastic wrap or a damp tea towel in a warm place for 1 to 2 hours to rise.

Knead dough on a floured board and shape into loafs or buns.

Leave to rise for another 30 mins.

Brush with a glaze of water.

Bake at 200C/400F for 30 mins until cooked through – longer for a large loaf or slightly shorter for smaller buns.

Alterations:

Swap out water for milk – milk creates a fluffier loaf, whereas water provides structure and creates a crustier loaf. Try activating yeast in ½ cup warm milk and adding 1 cup water to create a good blend. Alter according to taste.

Add honey or sugar to your yeast mixture to add sweetness and give the yeast some more food to help it thrive.

Add 2 Tbsp or so of olive oil to your dough to alter the flavour and create a longer lasting soft texture.

Try rolling your dough instead of kneading and roll it into a pinwheel or twist it into different shapes.

Glaze your bread with water, milk, oil or a beaten egg and see how it changes.

Boil your dough before baking for a more bagel-like texture.

Try adding spices, herbs, seeds or dried fruit to your dough and find which flavours you like.

Buy different types of flour and try blending them to see how they alter the properties of your loaf. Wholegrain and stone-ground flour are heavier and will create a denser, more characterful loaf but they may need some more assistance to rise – Often mixing more than one kind of flour together is a good way to get both the flavour and the texture you are after.

Try altering the amount of time you let your bread rise and the location. The temperature can impact rising a lot, so hot water cupboards or safe locations near a fire might help if the temperature of your home is fairly low.

Yoghurt Flatbread

As simple as it sounds, this two-ingredient flatbread can be whipped up quick and easy to provide extra sustenance to a meal like curry or soup or be served with hummus for an afternoon snack. Alter the ratios according to your preference and add extra ingredients like nigella seeds or vanilla essence for an extra pop of flavour.

Base recipe:
1 cup flour
1 cup natural/Greek yoghurt

Mix together until combined, add extra flour or liquid until smooth.

Roll flat and fry in a frypan on each side until lightly toasted.

Garden Smoothie

Using fresh fruit, veg and herbs from your garden can be a great way to start the day – or provide a nice cool drink to keep you motivated with your gardening!

Leafy greens like kale and spinach are very healthy additions, but growing herbs like mint add flavour and make your smoothie entirely more enjoyable. Using a bulky fruit like apples or pears with plant-based milk or yoghurt makes a great base, but a sprig of mint can really finish it off.

Growing berries can also make your smoothies colourful as well as tasty, with only a few needed for maximum flavour.

One banana, a hunk of peanut butter, cinnamon and fresh whole milk makes one heck of a good smoothie base, but adding in some blueberries takes it out of this world. If you can't grow your own, consider keeping a bag of frozen berries on hand.

Chia seeds add more substance, with only a teaspoon or so needed to make your smoothie a filling, stomach-satisfying light meal.

Cleaning

Cleaning is one of those tasks in life that inspires strong emotions – and often negative ones. I think this is in part due to the fact it feels like a Sisyphean endeavour: never-ending, labourious and in the great scheme of things, utterly futile.

There is also a poisonous bitterness around the division of labour and the fact that despite the threat that robots are rising up to take our jobs, they seem in large part to be letting advances in lessening domestic labour flag behind. If the AI age resulted in automation of labour but left income and leisure alone, I don't think we would have so many complaints.

The International Labour Organization has

measured unpaid domestic and care work and has found that over 16 billion hours are devoted to it every day.[10] Of this, 76% of the total daily hours falls on the shoulders of women and girls. If these hours were paid the monetary value that they are worth, in some countries it would be up to 40% of their GDP – and this is based on conservative estimates.[11]

The cottagecore aesthetic is largely void of labourious cleaning, as it is based on an idyllic daydream. In the words of James Baldwin's viral TikTok sound: "Darling... I have no dream job. I do not dream of labour."

Like many things cottagecore, this is held paradoxically alongside a sustainably maintained home that isn't filled with trash or falling to pieces. The cottagecore approach to cleaning requires both simplification and a shift in perspective around what cleaning means to you and how you relate to it. We'll look at the two main elements of this – minimization and appreciation – and consider a few ways to arrange your home to transform cleaning from a burden into a form of wellbeing.

---

[10] https://ilostat.ilo.org/topics/unpaid-work/measuring-unpaid-domestic-and-care-work/
[11] Ibid.

Minimization

One of the first and most obvious things to help you keep a well-maintained home is to have less stuff. Getting rid of things that don't fit your vibe, storing things you want to keep but don't want on display, and rotating seasonal items can help you keep the things that you want accessible – and still leave space to live.

Hand-washing your dishes as you go can help keep your kitchen bench clean and your space free of clutter and used mugs or plates. You won't find them lying around your house if you have your one favourite mug or teacup that you keep returning to.

Wooden serving boards – rather than having a variety of platters (unless you really love them), having a natural chopping board you can cut and serve food on cuts down on how many dishes you're making. If you wax your boards, they don't absorb moisture and only require a fast wipe down with cold water.

Effective cleaners – using quality cleaning supplies like ScrubDaddy sponges and Barkeeper's Friend can cut down the amount of elbow grease you need to use to keep your spaces clean and free up your time to enjoy life. I highly recommend the ScrubMommy sponge, as it is dual sided and can be used for pretty much everything.

Appreciating your materials

Feeling a personal connection to the products you use can help you to feel grounded, placing yourself within the context of both history and your own personal journey. I feel as though understanding where I fit within history gives me both appreciation for the advances humankind has made that we have all inherited, as well as a sense of self-forgiveness and grace for my own limitations.

One of the charms of watching lifehack videos on TikTok is that we can feel that the content creator is sharing a secret with us – wisdom paid for by their own mistakes and failures, and by sharing their newfound knowledge we can benefit from the time or labour-saving tips and tricks.

History is much like this as well, as every item in your home has a story, an inventor and a whole chain of development behind it.

ScrubDaddy's history is easily accessible, as the product was introduced on Shark Tank and the original pitch is available readily on YouTube – and there are many creators out there like @aurikatariina who make using their products in videos fun. Plenty of other brands like to share their stories, like Will&Able which features pictures of their staff members on their packaging. Craft fairs similarly allow you to meet craftspeople like soap makers and give you a personal connection to the people making the products you use.

Having handmade cloths – either made by yourself, gifted by a friend or bought from a local craftsperson – also provides you with materials that have pleasant connotations when you pick them up. If you have old rags that don't clean well, are disintegrating or just give you 'yuck' vibes when you pick them up, it might be time to chuck them in the bin and give yourself an upgrade.

Isolated ingredients also have a rich history of development that gives a fascinating view into the development of our products and how people lived before, through and after industrialization. Bicarbonate of soda (aka soda ash aka baking soda) is one of these ingredients – and a staple in every cottagecore home.

Baking soda is used in just about everything from

cleaning supplies to toothpaste to baking to home-science volcano projects – and its use can be traced back through different forms all the way to Ancient Egypt.

Long before we were using baking soda to try and absorb stinky foot smells out of our sneakers, the Ancient Egyptians were looking for a solution to keeping mummified bodies dry – an important preservative to protect their bodies in perfect condition for their journey to the afterlife. They discovered their answer in a sodium compound called Natron, which was to be found in dry salt-lake beds. Through experimentation with this compound, the Egyptians found that it had a multitude of uses. It was super effective at cleaning around the home, an effective personal soap when mixed with olive oil, a natural toothpaste and an anti-septic mouthwash when diluted with water. They also used it to create a sootless flame torch that would prevent damage to its environment and used it in the chemical process for glassmaking.[12]

---

[12] Sutherland, Diane, Jon Sutherland, Liz Keevill, Kevin Eyres, and Maria Costantino. *Household Hints, Naturally: Garden, Beauty, Health, Cooking, Laundry, Cleaning*. (Flame Tree Publishing, 2019), 6-7.

Potash was used as early as the Bronze Age for similar uses, including making soaps, ceramics, glass and in the bleaching process for textiles. Potash is actually not a single product or compound, but a range of potassium compounds depending on the source – and is where the word 'potassium' finds its root. One form of potash is still mined today, more commonly known as table salt!

Cleaning the bath...?

...or doing home science?

In the 14th century wood-derived potash was used throughout Europe for soap and the production of yarn. This was produced by running water over wood ash and evaporating the water to reveal the useful compound – unfortunately, this meant that a huge amount of woodland was burnt to produce it, and it proved unsustainable to meet demand. In 1783 the French Academy of Sciences set a challenge with a large prize to anyone who could produce a simple and economical method to produce soda ash. Nicholas LeBlanc found the solution, completing his experiments in 1790 and being awarded the 15-year patent in 1791, but the French Revolutionary Wars prevented him from receiving the prize money and saw his factories being confiscated.[13]

Meanwhile, in 1790 Samuel Hopkins was awarded the first US patent for inventing a new method for refining potash and pearlash. While potash was used for industrial purposes, pearlash was finer and was fit for human consumption. This meant it could be used as a leavening agent in baking bread![14] Pearlash appeared in several recipe books in the early 1800s, although it had a strong flavour and was replaced as modern baking soda and baking powder

---

[13] https://www.britannica.com/biography/Nicolas-Leblanc
[14] https://invention.si.edu/invention-stories/licensing-first-us-patent

became available in the 1840s.

In the 1830s Austin Church, an American doctor, experimented with different ways to refine sodium bicarbonate to great success. He left his medical practice and went into production with his brother-in-law, John Dwight, naming their high-grade sodium bicarbonate 'Saleratus' – or aerated salt.

Figure 11 Dwight's Saleratus Trading Card, 1870

Over the next few decades the word 'saleratus' fell out of favour and 'baking soda' replaced it. It remains a preferred almost-all-purpose component in kitchens and laundries as well as science labs across the world.

Each and every product in your home has a rich

history like this behind it, so when you're cleaning think of the gift and the rich wealth of knowledge that you've inherited. At the very least, it might provide a distraction until you're done cleaning the bath.

Appreciating Nature

Your relationship with nature is a key element of a cottagecore lifestyle. Much of modern life removes us from our environment, but there have been many studies that show being in nature is extremely important for your mental health.

The joys of 'forest bathing', of grounding yourself by walking barefoot and of enjoying scents and sounds from nature can be very healing, especially if you have been burned out.

In the next chapter we will have a closer look into the history of botany and how people's relationships with plants shifted in the 18th and 19th centuries, but for now consider your own personal relationship with nature. Many people find as life has shifted to more urban environments and as more time is spent in the digital realm, it gets harder and harder to feel a connection with nature. Exposure to the elements – both the warmth of sunshine and the chill of the wind – is reduced as we spend more time indoors, particularly in climate-controlled environments, and time spent engaging our senses with plants is reduced and, in many instances, replaced with artificial reproductions. How many of the scents you are surrounded with are chemical imitations? Do you have any plastic plants in your office? Can you see any greenery from your home? How often do you go outside and engage with it physically?

Gardening is one of the most obvious ways to improve your relationship with nature. There are so many kinds of gardens that you could try – a kitchen garden with vegetables you can take from earth to plate, an herb garden to make your cooking more lively and interesting, a tea garden using the flavours you would like to incorporate into your own dried teas, or a flower garden for pure pleasure and to bring wildlife closer to your home. You could choose one, or you could combine a few ideas into your dream garden.

Take a moment to look at your space, and to think about what kinds of things you would like to grow. One excellent way of identifying plants that will do well in your climate is to take a walk around your neighbourhood and see what plants are thriving. Take photos, make notes in a journal, and if you ask permission from the owners, you may be allowed to take cuttings or seeds at the appropriate time in the season.

Local botanic gardens also often have an excellent selection of different varieties of plants, so they are a great place to go idea-shopping – even better than Instagram as what you see online may not thrive in your specific location.

Annual plants are a great way to feel connected to the shifting seasons. Many low maintenance gardens prefer perennial plants, which can be useful for structural plants like hedges or shrubs, but seasonal annual plants while high maintenance can be an experience that feels totally different. Monet's famous garden was filled with annual plants that need to be replanted every season. Some things, while high effort, provide a beauty that is unmatched. They also provide a fantastic variety of blooms for bouquets or dried flowers.

The most important thing is that you design your garden to fit your values and what you desire from it. You will spend a lot of time in it, so turn it into something you love.

If you don't have an outdoor garden, you can still introduce greenery and plants into your home in other ways. House plants are easy to propagate and care for – many of them only need a little water once a week or so. The main thing with indoor plants is to learn their body language as if they are unhappy, their location, sun exposure, temperature or watering/nutritional needs may need to be addressed – and they may need to have their roots trimmed every couple of years. Once you've grown accustomed to your plants (and it may take a few plant deaths before you get there), you'll be able to recognize what they need by the state of their foliage.

If that is too much commitment, you could also look into sprouting seeds or growing microgreens to use in your cooking. They're pleasant to look at, disposable when you eat them, and have a very low bar to entry.

What do you currently do with your food scraps? Having a composting system is a great way to complete the cycle and build on your relationship with nature. So is feeding the birds, bugs or other critters which come to visit you.

Generally speaking, it's not a good idea to throw meat outside lest you attract rats (or other animals you don't want), and if you're in an area with snakes you may want to be careful where you leave food as they can be attracted if they find a place that mice frequent. Knowing what animals you are around will help you know what food offerings will be eaten and by which kinds of animals.

Spend a few moments outside doing a grounding activity and opening your awareness to what creatures may be in your back yard.

My grandma spent a huge amount of her time in her garden, and part of her ethos of living generously was by giving empty jam jars to the insects instead of washing them. She used to hang them upside down on garden stakes 'so the bugs can have the last licks.'

You could also spend some time making a bug hotel in your garden or constructing areas that water can pool to create good drinking spots for visiting creatures.

If you have the space and are zoned for animals, you could also look into getting chickens or quail for fresh eggs and wonderful company.

Propagating plants is extremely easy. Some plants, like rosemary and lavender, will often root suspended in a glass of water. Other plants may want a helping hand with some rooting hormone powder and seed raising mix. This is an extremely cheap way to get started, especially as many people will be happy to allow you to take cuttings for free.

Ideas to get you started:

- Grow microgreens in your kitchen.
- Plant some herbs that you would like to cook with (parsley, sage, rosemary, thyme, basil etc).
- Get a potplant and watch it grow – learn its preferences for light and water.
- Plant some bee and butterfly friendly plants like lavender and swan plants.
- Build a bug hotel and install it in your garden.
- Make a watering hole for insects and birds – a dish with a few stones in it is perfect, providing a place for critters to stand and drink without drowning.

- Install a chair outside in a sheltered location and give yourself the space to enjoy your environment.
- Install a birdfeeder and bring birdsong closer to your environment.
- Take a census of the wildlife in your area. You can use tracking tunnels and ink cards to capture footprints of sneaky animals with peanut butter as a lure.
- Locate parks and nature walks close to your home and visit them regularly.

Botany and The Flower Language

Floriography, or *'the language of flowers'*, was an 18th Century craze that has seen a recent revival in popular culture. Mary Wortley Montagu (1689-1762) is one of the key figures who introduced the concept to Europe through her letters describing the practice she had discovered during her travels in Turkey. Objects — primarily but not limited to flowers — were given as gifts encoding symbolic messages to the recipient.

This idea developed and was often romanticized as a way in which women in Turkey would communicate with each other secretly, although the accuracy of some of the tales is suspect at best. Nevertheless, floriography caught the attention and inspired the imaginations of people across the world and developed into a language that was not only used in personal relationships but became infused in literature and art – for both men and women.

It developed alongside a transition that was occurring in the role of women in science, as women fought to be taken seriously in the field of botany. While women were often associated with plants, and particularly their uses in healing, cooking and the domestic realm throughout history, their role as experts in the field of plants became contentious as botany became a 'serious subject of modern scientific enquiry' in the late 18th century and early 19th century.

The study of plants had been considered one of the few branches of scientific study that was also a socially acceptable ladylike pursuit, with women studying, painting, embroidering, illustrating and writing books on plants. One such book, *A Curious Herbal (1737-39)* was published in two volumes containing five hundred illustrations of plants – etched, engraved and hand-coloured by Elizabeth Blackwell. This was a study of plants complete with physical descriptions for identification, the time and place of growth and flowering, 'it's common uses in Physick', as well as the ordinary names of the plant in multiple languages including English, French, German, Spanish, Dutch, Greek and Latin.[15] The amount of expertise and effort to achieve such a project is absolutely tremendous.

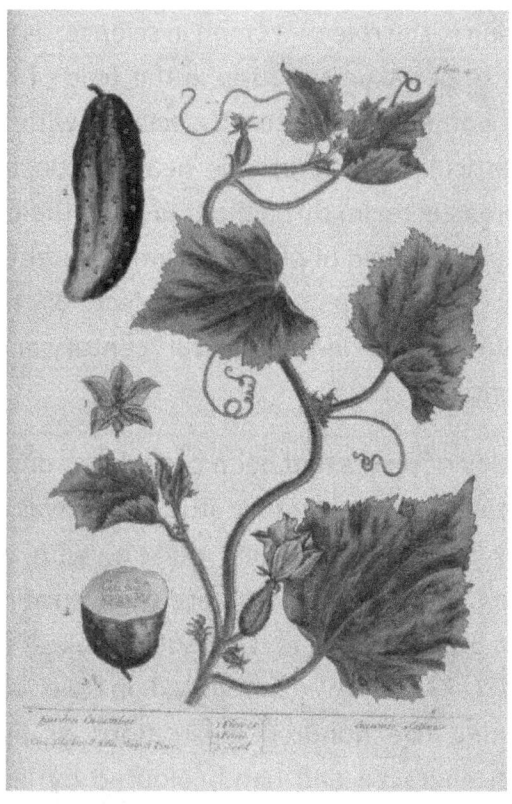

Figure 12 Garden Cucumber by Elizabeth Blackwell, 1737.

---

[15] Blackwell, Elizabeth. *A Curious Herbal*. Samuel Harding, 1737.

Women also incorporated floral illustrations into fashion to striking effect. The portrait of Anne Shippen Willing (Mrs. Charles Willing) wearing a floral dress made of silk brocade is an excellent example of the impact of fashion on history. The dress itself was designed by Anna Maria Garthwaite of Spitalfields Silk, a designer who has left such a mark during her 33-year career that she has a Blue Plaque commemorating her efforts.[16] Garthwaite likely would have received no formal training, but would have spent time learning from the master weavers and traders of the persecuted Huguenot communities who brought new skills in silk weaving and designing to Britain in the 1680s.[17] While the Huguenots and their new silk processes were initially unwelcome by many traditional weavers who felt threatened by them, the resulting designs became a subject of British pride as they travelled across the globe. In the peak of her career, Garthwaite produced eighty designs per year, and her textiles have been found in the UK, wider

---

[16] Anna Maria Garthwaite's plaque can be found at 2 Princelet Street, Spitalfields, London, E1 6QH, London Borough of Tower Hamlets.
[17] https://www.english-heritage.org.uk/visit/blue-plaques/anna-maria-garthwaite/

Europe and North America.[18] Garthwaite's dress design pictured in Anne Willing's portrait is the subject of a book of its own by historian Zara Anishanslin, *Portrait of a Woman in Silk.*[19]

Figure 13 Anne Shippen Willing (Mrs. Charles Willing) by Robert Feke, 1746.

---

[18] Ibid.
[19] *Portrait of a Woman in Silk: Hidden Histories of the British Atlantic World,* Zara Anishanslin, Yale University Press, 2016.

The blending of science and art can be seen throughout every strain that either appears, and also always entangled in social history and disenfranchisement of class, race and gender. While botany has of course existed as long as humans have identified different types of plants (delicious, useful, poisonous, able to be cultivated etc) it exploded in popularity as both a serious pursuit and a kind of 'polite entertainment' in the 18th Century.

Botany was also an attractive past-time for working class men, much to the consternation of some of the elite. Some botanists readily recognized the efforts and achievements of novice practitioners, while others made a concerted effort to snub those they saw as amateurs sullying the science with soil-stained fingers. Guides to botany from the period often emphasize that a line must be drawn between a serious botanist and a mere home gardener. Despite the derision some experienced for their efforts, plant enthusiasts persisted in their engagement with all things floral. Several different influences converged to push botany into its prominent state, although the paths it has taken have branched and reconnected in a spiderweb of science, art, and activism.

In 1735, Swedish biologist and physician Carl Linnaeus published his book on biological taxonomy, *Systema Naturae,* which categorized plants and broke down information about them into an accessible format. While women were active participants and keenly invested in the plant world, they were usually excluded from higher education including learning Latin – the language employed in much of the scientific world. The accessibility of the Linnean System and subsequent publications designed to assist women in becoming interesting conversational partners and informed teachers to their 'little people' (insert eye-roll here), provided women with opportunities to study and discover the secrets of plants for themselves. While many of their discoveries were overlooked or purposefully snubbed[20], women infused their knowledge into art, craft and literature as well as the language of flowers whose symbolism has cross-pollinated much of the Victorian world.

It should also be noted that Linnaeus, while popular at the time, was not without critics. His approach to taxonomy was heavily influenced by religious ideals and contemporary tendencies which coloured the way he divided the world, but he also went against the grain to great outrage. Linnaeus divided the world into the three kingdoms of nature: animal, vegetable, and mineral. The decision to class

---

[20] Ie: Linnaeus' dismissal of Jane Colden's contributions.

humans as animals was shocking and an unwelcome concept to some. He further classified humans into four groups: Europaeus albus: European white; Americanus rubescens: American reddish; Asiaticus fuscus: Asian tawny; Africanus niger: African black. From here, much like Hogwarts Houses, he attributed each variety of human with certain traits, with Europeans exhibiting "light, wise, inventor" traits and Africans "sly, sluggish, neglectful."[21]

His classifications have, of course, since been dismissed as complete and utter bullshit, but did contribute to the development of scientific racism that expanded throughout the 18th and 19th century and can still be recognized in modern eugenics movements today.

The prevalence of Western taxonomy and modes of categorization as one of the foundational blocks of modern science is also being revisited as people are recognizing just how much indigenous knowledge and feminine knowledge has been overlooked and excluded. Much of the time indigenous knowledge has been passed down by oral tradition, while women's observations were recorded in the more familiar styles of diaries, journals, letters, poems and artwork. These strategies have caused them to

---

[21] https://www.linnean.org/learning/who-was-linnaeus/linnaeus-and-race

be largely overlooked by official publications while still transmitting ideas through social exchange.[22]

The publication of *Systema Naturae* was still extremely impactful despite any shortcomings however, as it inspired plant enthusiasts and scientists across Europe and America to begin categorizing and recording plant species anywhere and everywhere. Home science labs were common among the wealthy, and plants were available everywhere, even for the financially impaired, making the bar to entry very low.

The Kew Gardens were also developed in 1759, with a collection that featured a massive diversity of plants from around the world. Prior to this, botanic gardens tended to have a medicinal focus, indicating what characteristics were seen as valuable. Kew Gardens, by comparison, reflects the interest in the exotic. Wealthy individuals would likewise build glass houses and amass their own collections of plants.[23] An interest in botany served many purposes: to exhibit one's wealth, to improve one's

---

[22] https://www.literatureandscience.org/issues/JLS_4_1/JLS_vol_4_no_1_GeorgeMartin.pdf

[23] Seaton, Beverly, *The Language of Flowers: A History,* (Charlottesville: University of Virginia Press) 1995.

mind, to stimulate the Empire or to express one's personality.

Window boxes and Wardian cases also became fashionable in the Victorian age and brought new ways for people to cultivate, enjoy and observe plants out of their natural environment. Window boxes and portable planters have of course been around for millennia. Pliny the Elder described these types of home garden at length in his work *Naturalis Historia*. The call for nature that brings plants into one's home is the same yearning found in cottagecore, the same philosophy exhibited in pastoralism and the same focus of the Arkadian dream – you can take the person out of the countryside, but they can always take a piece of the countryside with them.

Wardian cases provided a solution to the needs of botanists wanting to transport plants on their travels, sometimes on long voyages. They were closed miniature glasshouses made with glazed glass panels, and often lined with layers of sphagnum moss. Coffee and tea plants, along with many other exotic varieties were transported safely out of their environment (with or without approval) this way to be established elsewhere. The modern versions of these cases are of course vivariums, terrariums, aquariums – and all manner of other 'ariums' – each of which is a specifically designed miniature habitat to contain a slice of nature.

Figure 14 Wardian Case, N. B. Ward.

With knowledge being passed around through the very accessible means of publications and more exotic types of plants being made available across the board, it's only natural that the development of people's relationships with plants developed in every direction according to personal passions and preferences.

The language of flowers, filled with whimsical imagination, was also heavily based on botanical study as the meanings of plants were developed according to their nature. Lavender, often used to mask scents, was symbolic of 'distrust.' Rhododendrons, due to their poisonous nature, were a sign of caution or could mean 'beware.' To receive a doubly poisonous bouquet of azaleas and rhododendrons could be a death threat – so beware when buying flowers for your beau!

The language of flowers permeated art and literature as well, with the time traveler in H.G. Wells' 1895 novel *'The Time Machine'*, landing in a bed of rhododendrons as he arrives in the future – a sign of caution and bad omen to the reader. Meanwhile, John Everett Millais' 1851-1852 painting *'Ophelia'* featured a multitude of symbolic flowers, some of which were never mentioned in the text by Shakespeare.

While the search through history and art can be endless, the main guiding question to ask yourself as you begin your own journey is what appeals to you?

Do you wish for a return to the native plants that would have grown in your area before the great plant migration began? If so, you'll find good company in the many people aiming to decolonize the environment.

Do you wish to understand the scientific nature of the plants around you, and how they grow and thrive? You've never lived in a better time, with education being more accessible than ever – and from much more reliable sources than Linnaeus!

Do you wish to enjoy the presence of flowers in art and literature and the many-layered messages they infuse? You may like my other book – The Flower Code by Laura Wolf[24] – which provides plenty of information and excerpts including two of the main lists of floriography: Kate Greenaway's list for Europe and the UK, and the American list from *'Gems of Deportment'*.

Take some time to consider your relationship with plants, and what you would like it to be in the future. If you have a botanic park or flower shop nearby, schedule a visit and take some time to notice what you notice.

---

[24] https://www.amazon.com/dp/B08N589816

Aromatherapy

Scents are incredibly powerful to our state of mind. An incredible amount of money has been invested in researching scent marketing and it has exploded into a $200 million dollar industry. Business giants have realized that aromas change people's emotions and behaviours and this impacts their willingness to spend as well as their brand loyalty. Different banks and hotels have their own signature scents that have been designed to promote ideas of luxury and wealth, while baby department stores might prefer a clean, powdery scent.

Aromas also have a strong connection to memory, and introducing familiar smells to your home and your daily routine can help recall positive memories associated with those scents.

On the other end of the scale, bad odors have been linked with increased rates of depression and aggression. Neurologist Dr. Alan Hirsch from the Smell & Taste Research and Treatment Foundation in Chicago has been widely quoted on his research in this area, although some of his work has proved controversial, particularly around some of his claims on the connection between smell and weight loss. You can read more about this here.[25]

While some elements of aromatherapy are not backed up with much scientific evidence, other parts of it are – as well as having deep roots in traditions and history which also have value. Even if you are dubious, it is important to not throw the baby out with the bathwater just as it's good to approach it with a touch of skepticism before investing huge amounts of money. It's also worth being aware that not every brand of oil is the same quality, and there can be a stark difference between a bottle of lavender oil and a bottle of lavender *scented* oil, so it's worth doing your research on brands before forking out. Despite some bad press,

---

[25] https://www.chicagotribune.com/2014/01/19/chicago-doctors-research-fails-federal-smell-test-2/

there are plenty of ways that aromatherapy can help enrich your life and you're going to be the one to decide on what works for you.

The main takeaway is to approach aromatherapy with curiosity and an open mind, but not to buy too much into extreme claims. Try things out and see what works for you personally and measure the impact on your own wellbeing. If it gives you joy or you find it helpful, it's a success regardless of the debates in peer reviewed journals. You are the best judge on your own sense of wellbeing.

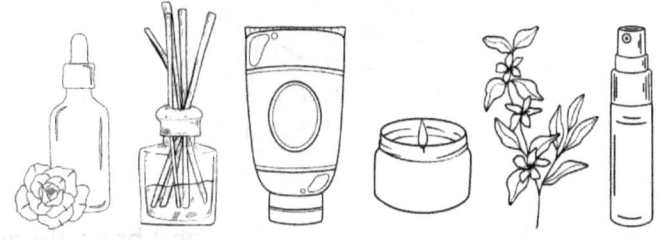

Personalizing scents

Take a moment to think about which smells relax you and which smells repulse you.

I can't stand the smell of old fruit or musty laundry. I *love* the smells of vanilla, lavender, cinnamon, sage, thyme, rosemary and fresh bread. Other floral scents like rose, I could take or leave. I used to like a few brands of perfume but now most of them give me a headache and just seem too synthetic to be enjoyable.

When you've identified the smells you enjoy, you can start incorporating them into your life. You could drip essential oils into your scarf or use it in your laundry to keep your clothes smelling nice. As a longer-lasting solution, you can create lavender or rose scented sachets to keep in your drawers.

You can plant the flowers you love and bring them into your house. If you have a favourite plant in the garden, you could place a chair or bench seat next to it to encourage yourself to sit out there with a cup of tea to enjoy it.

You could scent different areas of your home with incense sticks, potpourri or diffusers to create different scent signatures for areas where you need a mental shift. If your bedroom smells like vanilla, you may associate that smell with rest and relaxation – whereas if you make your office smell like eucalyptus, or another invigorating smell. When you sit down at your desk to work, your brain will already be processing that you're in a different zone and you can get yourself into work-mode. You can achieve the same affect with herbal teas, reserving chamomile for just before bed and other blends or flavours for different times of day when you need energy, focus or relaxation.

You may want to use cooking or baking to scent your home as well – many people love the smell of freshly baked cookies, so much that people will often bake them before an open home to help sell their house. Even when my pantry is full, I will sometimes still bake cookies and box them up to give away as the smell of baking can be a reward in itself. Don't tell my landlord, but I also often do a bit of baking the morning before a rental inspection.

Scenting your body can also provide a positive smell that you can take with you. Shampoo, deodorant, perfume or scented moisturizers can achieve this effect, so have a think about which products you use and if you like the smell of them or if you have chosen them without taking that into consideration. Those smells will follow you around all day, so it's worth selecting ones that you actually like.

Take a moment to do a grounding exercise and identify what smells you have within your house. Move to different rooms around your house and see what scents you can identify. Are there any that you like? Are there any negative scents that you would like to alter?

Do you have any strong memories associated with scents? What did your childhood home smell like? Are there any identifiable flowers that stand out in your memory? If not, could you schedule a trip to a plant store or a public garden so you can consciously go and smell the flowers to see which ones you like? Don't forget that herb gardens are also a great choice and that flowers aren't your only option. Touching the leaves of a mint or thyme plant releases a strong scent, so consider the tactile element of your ideal garden.

Take photos of the plants you like and look into what you will need to help them thrive in your home environment. You could get yourself a greenhouse or raised bed, or you could start one plant at a time and take your time as you get to know them and how to care for them.

Potpourri

Potpourri is a fantastic way to cover bad odours and/or introduce positive ones. While you can buy potpourri pre-mixed and scented, you can also very easily make your own.

Take flowers and petals from your garden, making sure that they are clean and intact before drying them. Strip foliage from the stems and hang them upside in your home in a low-humidity area. When selecting flowers, don't use too many different fragrances – while fragrant flowers are very effective, combining too many can sometimes clash and result in a clash of perfumes.

Once dry, mix through with a few drops of essential oil and place in a bowl to scent your room or in bags to scent your drawers. When the scent fades, refresh it with another few drops of your favourite essential oil.

Making lavender bags is very easy. Organza bags with ribbon ties are a very easy option that require no sewing and make it easy to refill or refresh the contents. Sewing a small pouch of dried flowers is also a very easy project for beginners as all you need is two rectangles, and the scent can be refreshed by dripping some essential oil onto it every season or so. Preferably use a natural fiber like cotton, or a mesh fabric like organza that will allow airflow, and make sure that your flowers are completely dry before use.

ESSENTIAL OILS BY COMMON USE

Allergies – Peppermint, lemon, lavender.

Anxiety, Depression and Stress – Patchouli, bergamot, juniper, lemon, frankincense, eucalyptus, lavender, rose.

Clarity/Meditation – Peppermint, frankincense.

Cleansing – Peppermint, clary sage, lemon.

Energy – Orange, pink grapefruit, lemon, bergamot, juniper.

Focus – Vetiver, lavender, sandalwood, rosemary.

Germs/Cleaning – Lavender, lemon, grapefruit, eucalyptus.

Sleep – Lavender, vetiver, chamomile.

Community

While the idea of cottagecore is sometimes characterized by the idea of the desire to run away and live in the woods, we do have to recognize that isolation and escapism may be a part of the fantasy but in reality, your connectedness with your community is an extremely important element of personal wellbeing. While there are some parts of your current social landscape that you may wish to reject, it is still possible and necessary to engage with your community on some level, but the ways in which that happens might be altered from your previous norms.

So much of modern socialization revolves around the online world. Swapping phone numbers, instant messaging, finding and following each other on social media… But when you can contact people *at any time*, the reality is that the convenience can give way to apathy and you can end up *never* talking to them or talking about utterly inconsequential things that make you feel like you haven't had a quality conversation in a very long time.

Taking a more intentional approach to your social life can give it a total rejuvenation. You may find that not everyone appreciates your old-school vibes (not everyone you write a letter will write one back, although I'm sure they'll appreciate reading it at the time), but people you might not expect could reciprocate and you could end up with deeper relationships as a result.

Letter Writing

Have a look through your contact list and think if there's anyone who is missing. Is there an old school friend or a distant cousin you would like to get in contact with from your childhood? Are there any people on your contact list who you haven't talked to that you would like to engage with?

Get yourself (or make yourself) an address book and create a hitlist of people you would like to send some letters by snail mail to. The contents of your letter don't need to be mind-blowing, but you could let them know you're thinking about them. I also like including sealed teabags in my letters, so the receiver can take a moment out of their busy life and feel calm and appreciated.

You also might want to include some stickers, a bookmark, a photo, or some dried pressed flowers from your garden. You might even want to post them something you've made, or a book you've read recently that they might enjoy.

Gifts

Well thought out gifts are worth more than gold – and handmade things are absolutely priceless. I still have a beanie crocheted by one of my friends at university and I think of her every time I see it.

She sat in the common room on campus crocheting every evening and made them for just about everyone she knew. Any of us who had money to spare would buy her wool, and people would let her know their preferred colours. We'd sit around and watch her crocheting, and others would bring their crafts out of their rooms as well – I ended up sitting with needle and thread mending people's pants some of those evenings as well. We had such a blast of a time getting to know each other, and all those memories are locked in those little loops of wool.

Baking or cooked meals are also a really impactful gift. When I had my babies, there was a full roster of women who dropped in meals for about three weeks. Even after that, there were a few mums in my community at that time who would bulk up their meals and set some aside to give away. Even if you aren't going through particularly hard times, it's always a pleasure to receive a delicious home-cooked meal (just check for allergies and preferences first).

There was also a group of women at one of my playgroups which got together once a month to share baking and recipes. They had an agreement between the 5 of them to make 5 batches worth of baking to share – they would taste one there, and the other 4 people would get a bundled-up share of baking to take home. Each person would leave with a full batch of baking *and* the recipe so they could test it on their families and decide if they wanted to put it into their cookbook.

Food is something amazing that brings people together in a way not much else does. Is there anyone you can think of that would appreciate an overnight couriered box of cookies?

Volunteering

Volunteering is a way to not only be generous with your time and skills, but to connect into your community and feel part of something bigger than yourself. There are also *so many* ways to volunteer, there's definitely something out there you can do that will add value to your life personally as well as your community.

If you are of a social disposition and have the time, you may want to go and volunteer regularly at a location with other people doing something you care about. If you're not particularly social but you still want to get out and about, you might consider volunteering at a pet shelter or cleaning up a local park, beach or outdoor space. Or if you're an introvert and want to stay mostly at home you could do something else – you could leave spare vegetables at the bottom of your driveway in a box for your community or drop them in a community pantry. You could rescue old books from op shops and rebind them to give away or make baby clothes and give them to midwives to hand on to mothers in need.

Take stock of your personality, your desires, your talents, and come up with some ideas that you could try.

Picnicking

Have a look around your local area and plan a picnic lunch in a nature-filled area. You could invite a friend, or just go by yourself. You could take a book, an SLR camera, a journal, or just yourself. With plenty of sustenance and entertainment, you could spend the whole day there or just take an hour to wander amongst the flowers or trees and listen to the birds.

Picnicking regularly is a great way to get out and see new areas that are off your regular paths, and having nice food is a great way to make an event out of it and cement it in your memory. While nailing down a day that people are free is often the hardest part of the process, I have rarely heard a straight 'no' to a picnic invitation.

Spirituality

The cottagecore aesthetic appeals to people from a wide range of spiritual beliefs who find common ground in the concept that connecting with nature is rejuvenating.

It is a little surreal to find the commonality between posts from the new age, pagan and wiccan communities that are also shared with Christian offshoots including the Utah farmgirl and #ChristianGirlAutumn trends — but perhaps it can also be encouraging that despite our different beliefs and expressions we share a lot of universal experiences, ideas and comforts.

It should be noted that there is a layer of toxicity that is present through the cottagecore adjacent "tradwife" trend, but that will be covered in "The Dark Side of Cottagecore" chapter later in this book. This chapter focuses instead on some of the concepts that lead to spiritual nourishment.

The very idea of spirituality can differ from person to person, but for the purpose of this exploration I will be separating it from any traditions related to religious practices and treating it as the more formless desire of concerning yourself with your spiritual self. This may feel like a connection between yourself and nature, your body and your 'soul', or your place within the world in a larger sense – whether it is the present moment, the far reaches of history, the universe itself or the story of your own personal life and journey.

Your idea of spirituality may change throughout the course of this book, and it may change several times throughout your life.

I find that over time I have come to relate more and more to Cat Stevens' song "Father & Son" as it doesn't limit itself to generational conversations but can also be applied to the changing perspectives that your future and past selves have with each other. Taylor Swift's *Folklore* also contributed towards many people's cottagecore journey when the surprise-drop album was released as the #cottagecore trend was accelerating, providing a perfect soundtrack for the movement. Her ballads explore ideas of self-reflection, meditation, self-exploration and the concept of myths and stories and how they impact ideas around your identity and the concept of the 'self'.

The complexities of societal pressure, of guilt and expectation, the shifting desires of your heart and the alternating ideas and priorities that come with different stages of your life journey shift your perspectives on things substantially, and for a lot of people their cottagecore journeys are an escape where they reconnect with themselves and recalibrate their spirit and body with who they are and what they want.

Cottagecore's ethos of splitting away from the 'grind' in order to find and nurture your true self resonate with these reflective popular songs which explore the paradoxical space where past, present, future, the world and the singular self all converge. The result, rather than excessive noise, is almost like sitting in the quiet of the eye of a hurricane.

The person who I am as a mother is very different to who I was as a maiden, and by the time I am a crone

I will look very different again.

The cottagecore retreat allows you to sit with who you are and gives you a moment of peace with yourself in the impermanent present.

Marie Antoinette in her idyllic hamlet exists in a separate moment from Marie Antoinette facing the riot of people leading her to her execution.

You in your present moment are allowed to separate yourself from your past, from any conflict in the future, from the chaos and concerns of the global newspapers. You, in this moment, are allowed to have a cup of tea and to listen to the wind, unhindered from any other thoughts or worries.

This desire for retreat and peace is nothing new, and dates back as far as we can track society. The poetry and essays of Ralph Waldo Emerson and Henry David Thoreau have been particularly impactful on the development of present expressions of Western naturalism as they reacted against the imposing march of civilization, government and the industrial revolution.

Emerson explores the relationship he has with

nature and his sense of self in his essay, *Nature*:

"In the woods, we return to reason and faith. There I feel that nothing can befall me in life,—no disgrace, no calamity, (leaving me my eyes,) which nature cannot repair. Standing on the bare ground,—my head bathed by the blithe air, and uplifted into infinite space,—all mean egotism vanishes. I become a transparent eye-ball; I am nothing; I see all; the currents of the Universal Being circulate through me; I am part or particle of God."[26]

Emerson described himself as aligning more with the Quakers than any other theological movement – a pacifist expression of Christianity characterized by the often loud or dramatic physical expressions of religious emotion such as trembling, 'quaking' or making noise as they made congress with the Holy Spirit or their 'inner light'.

One thing that set Emerson as well as the Quaker movement apart, was the emphasis on rejecting prescribed norms and looking inwardly for self-reliance. The Quakers, originally known as the 'Society of Friends', met staunch opposition as they

---

[26] R. W. Emerson, Chapter I, *Nature,* Boston & Cambridge: James Munroe And Company, 1849.

rejected ordained ministry, oaths and rites including tithes, and military service.[27] The Quakers looked inwardly to their own existence for their connection with and experience of God and saw no need for a wider organizational system like Catholicism or Anglicanism.

Emerson, likewise, looked to this philosophy of God, nature, and self-reliance for the ultimate experience of feeling at peace. His philosophies in naturalism and transcendentalism can be traced throughout the 1800s and into both the modern homesteading movement as well as the hippy anti-war movements in the mid to late 1900s.

Thoreau was a great friend of Emerson, and their philosophies intertwined to great effect. Thoreau famously retreated to a cabin in the woods that he had built himself on Emerson's land where he compiled his literary masterpiece, *Walden*. He lived a #cottagecore life, communing with nature and being one with his environment, spending time meditating and attending to his most basic needs. Thoreau notes the difference between his simple lifestyle and that of the labour of farmers who toil the land, which highlights the need for the rustic

---

[27] https://www.britannica.com/biography/George-Fox

cottagecore life without the burden of labour – his ideal existence is more like the idylls of Theocritus with the reclining goatherds resting in contemplation than the image of a TikTok #tradwife glorifying the labours of love:

"I see young men, my townsmen, whose misfortune it is to have inherited farms, houses, barns, cattle, and farming tools; for these are more easily acquired than got rid of. Better if they had been born in the open pasture and suckled by a wolf, that they might have seen with clearer eyes what field they were called to labor in. Who made them serfs of the soil? Why should they eat their sixty acres, when man is condemned to eat only his peck of dirt? Why should they begin digging their graves as soon as they are born? They have got to live a man's life, pushing all these things before them, and get on as well as they can. How many a poor immortal soul have I met well nigh crushed and smothered under its load, creeping down the road of life, pushing before it a barn seventy-five feet by forty, its Augean stables never cleansed, and one hundred acres of land, tillage, mowing, pasture, and wood-lot! The portionless, who struggle with no such unnecessary inherited encumbrances, find it labor enough to subdue and cultivate a few cubic feet of flesh.

But men labor under a mistake. The better part of the man is soon plowed into the soil for compost. By a seeming fate, commonly called necessity, they are employed, as it says in an old book, laying up treasures which moth and rust will corrupt and thieves break through and steal. It is a fool's life, as they will find when they get to the end of it, if not before."[28]

His reflection on the idea of a home and housekeeping further sets him apart from the idea of the subject that often makes up homesteading or aesthetic décor channel content and more firmly into the minimalist ideal of naturalism:

"At present our houses are cluttered and defiled with it, and a good housewife would sweep out the greater part into the dust hole, and not leave her morning's work undone. Morning work! By the blushes of Aurora and the music of Memnon, what should be man's morning work in this world? I had three pieces of limestone on my desk, but I was terrified to find that they required to be dusted daily, when the furniture of my mind was all undusted still, and I threw them out the window in disgust. How,

---

[28] Henry David Thoreau, *Walden and On the Duty of Civil Disobedience,* 1854.

then, could I have a furnished house? I would rather sit in the open air, for no dust gathers on the grass, unless where man has broken ground."[29]

Thoreau challenges the idea of maintaining a house or a life when your spirit remains unaddressed. What do you lose out on when you are so busy dusting your knick-knacks that you let your mind sit foggy and undusted? If you gave your mind time to clear and your spirit time to recalibrate, what things would you see with new clarity?

It's also important to note that while Emerson and Thoreau's writings are inspirational in their deep reflection, they also did not remain in one state for the duration of their lives. Thoreau lived in his cabin for two years and two months, and during his later years shifted his focus towards activism. Thoreau also would not have been able to live his #cottagecore life if not for the fact he was allowed a space of land in which to build his dwelling. In the end, we all have to live in the context which we exist, which may include obligations to family, rent or mortgages. Figuring out which of these things are unconscious defaults we return to and which are actually necessary is a process which can take a long

---

[29] Ibid.

time to untangle.

Reflection is an important part of your journey, and regular reflective practices can help you continue to find balance, purpose and fulfillment in life. Leaving your environment like going on a hike, sitting in the garden or going to live in the woods can be a great reflective experience - but few people who remove themselves into a state of hermitage remain there forever. Which reflective practices you find useful will vary from person to person.

During my degree in Theology, I did a paper on spirituality which explored the different ways people connected to God and themselves. While ideas around God/god(/s)/consciousness/the universe/nature vary across belief systems, the concepts of spiritual exploration and trial and error are fairly similar across the board.

My degree was done in a Christian college and therefore came from a Christian perspective, so the analogies I have are largely based in the Christian tradition and church history. During my four years of intensive spiritual exploration and analysis I looked at the branching expressions of Christianity in all its forms – Greek Orthodoxy, Catholicism, Anglicanism, Methodism, Presbyterianism, Pentecostalism, and the teachings of various monasteries and the Desert Fathers in early Christian mysticism.

The more I learned the more I realized I did not know, and the more I came to realize that we have a tendency to overcomplicate things until we cannot see the trees for the forest. There is a freedom in letting go of the Great Unknown in favour of sitting in the present to 'be as we are'.

Whether there are candles or no candles, music or silence, a coherent theology or a quiet vibration of your soul in your body, very little changes. From Theocritus in 300BC to Thoreau in 1854 to ourselves in the present, very little has changed. There is a universal sense of mortality, doom, immediacy, eternity, peace and life that we all share – something that connects us through stars, poetry and watching the flowers grow.

Even after years of study and personal soul-searching I can offer you no specific guidance, but I can offer you some opportunities for self-reflection – it is up to you what you find you relate to, and what you find sticks. Do not worry if they are only temporary changes – if Thoreau is able to walk away from his cabin at Walden, you're allowed to close your journal and put it on the shelf.

Spiritual Practices:

- **Silence** – take some time to sit in silence for at least five minutes a day. Let your mind drift and embrace the time in-between. This moment is not for active thoughts but sitting with yourself until the ripples on the shore of your mind find stillness.
- **Being barefoot in nature** – allowing yourself to feel at one with the earth, letting the soles of your feet touch grass or having your toes crunch in the sand, this practice allows you to find your place back in the physical world at your mammalian core self.
- **Prayer** – putting your feelings, desires and regrets into spoken words either to a cosmic being, God or just letting them loose into the world, prayer can take many forms. Speaking from the heart with an original composition or reciting written prayers or psalms, weaving unspoken feelings and thoughts together can provide clarity, relief or reinforcement.
- **Song** – it is no wonder so many religions and cultural practices include elements of song, as it resonates deeply within your body and helps to express feelings, lift moods and

expel energy to leave you refreshed and ready for new things. Whether you sing formless tunes, traditional hymns or songs by Taylor Swift, they can all be considered spiritual practices.

- **Meditation** – if silence is not appealing, you can take a guided meditation to instructions on an app or to music. You can also meditate on a piece of writing, repeating it over and over in your mind or on paper, finding new meaning as you turn it over like a stone in your hand.
- **Yoga** – while some people treat yoga as exercise-only, many people find benefit in following it as a spiritual practice. There are many apps, lessons on YouTube and in-person groups with varying approaches.
- **Journalling** – keeping a journal can help you sort through your thoughts and feelings, but also provides a record to look back and reflect on your journey and growth over time.

Forgiveness and Gratitude

One thing living with a chronic illness has taught me is that your personal mindset can make all the difference between misery and joy. Life is full of difficulties and injustices that often push us towards escapist dreams like the idyllic cottagecore aesthetic, but the difference between the unattainable dream and real joy is a shift in mindset and expectation.

Learning to let go of negative things in our past and present and hold life lightly in our hands with a spirit of gratitude can shift the entire axis of our reality.

The idea of forgiveness is something people often have a difficult relationship with as it is often misused and abused, encouraging the victim to continue to tolerate intolerable behaviour. When done well, forgiveness doesn't allow injustice to be perpetuated, but instead allows us to step away from bitterness and the ongoing suffering that comes along with reliving events and relying on a sense of closure which may never be realized.

In *The Book of Joy*, Archbishop Desmond Tutu describes the importance of forgiveness:

"Forgiveness is the only way to heal ourselves and be free from the past... Without forgiveness, we remain tethered to the person who harmed us. We are bound to the chains of bitterness, tied together, trapped. Until we forgive the person who harmed us, that person will hold the keys to our happiness, that person will be our jailor. When we forgive, we take back control of our own fate and our feelings. We become our own liberator."[30]

While the Archbishop has many stories of reconciliation after shocking levels of wrongdoing that are detailed in *The Book of Joy,* it's also important to note that forgiveness doesn't always have to be accompanied by reconciliation.

---

[30] Lama, Dalai, Desmond Tutu, and Douglas Abrams. *The Book of Joy*. Hutchinson Publishing, 2016, 234-235.

Sometimes forgiveness can be as much as letting go of the desire for karmic revenge and leaving the perpetrator to their fate.

Some situations it is advisable to go through the court system and seek justice, especially if there is damage that needs to be repaid or there is danger of continued harm to yourself or others – but in some situations justice may not prevail. It is also impossible to extract an apology out of a person who is dead, doesn't remember the event, or is unwilling or unrepentant. At some stage you will need to ask yourself how much of your life you will continue to dedicate to the damage they have caused, and where the line is you will draw before dedicating that time and emotional space to your own growth, enjoyment and improvement. That process might need to be accompanied by therapy.

It is also important to remember that trauma can leave a lasting impact on your physical body that is not removed with forgiveness. Forgiveness is also not a one-time-fix-all, as there can be ongoing grief and anxiety that need revisiting many times.

Bessel van der Kolk's best-selling book *The Body Keeps the Score*, shifted the conversation around trauma with his research on PTSD and how it impacts people who have experienced trauma as well as the people around them. Van der Kolk explains that self-awareness is at the core of recovery for trauma victims. People who have experienced trauma often become afraid of feeling itself, and it is no surprise that many of them resort to solutions like alcoholism, drugs or dissociative habits that dull or distract from facing up to the feelings that they find utterly unbearable.[31] He also explains that over the past two decades treatment for trauma has often resorted to some form of systematic desensitization, with the goal of making the person less reactive to certain emotions. This, he says, has been shown to lead to an overall blunting of emotional sensitivity. He suggests instead, an approach of integration, where the traumatic event is put into the correct place in the person's story arc of their lives.[32]

This fits in well with my theory of forgiveness – not ignoring or trying to delete the person or the event, but placing the wrongdoing, the trauma, the negativity, back into the place within your history it

---

[31] van der Kolk, Bessel, M.D. *The Body Keeps the Score*. Penguin Books, 2015, 249.
[32] Ibid., 267.

belongs.

Many people attracted to cottagecore are not seeking the escapist dream with the goal of becoming numb. Everything about the aesthetic is a delight to the senses – the flavours, the smells, the sensations of being out in a meadow on a sunny day with a light breeze rushing through the trees.

The cottagecore dream is not an escape from feeling, it is an escape to a place where it is safe to feel.

Focusing on small pleasures can have a positive effect on both your mental health and your sensory nervous system which is wired into your stress responses. Your memory has strong associations with certain inputs and learning what they are can be an incredible help.

For me, the smell of vanilla reminds me of good times baking in the kitchen – both as a child and an adult – so I have incorporated that into my home as much as I can. I have vanilla scented reeds in my lounge and bathroom, and I add vanilla essence to my cleaning products which leaves surfaces smelling pleasant rather than of vinegar after a wipe-down.

My theory of forgiveness in practice gives space to make the present your own, and my theory of gratitude brings appreciation and enjoyment into every moment it can fit into.

Marcus Aurelius' *Meditations* begins with a recollection of the things he has learned from each person in his life who has made a positive contribution: his father, his mother, his grandparents, his teachers, siblings and friends. He based his philosophy first on what he has received and then on his subsequent lessons and decisions on how to better himself. While many Roman emperors – and modern-day leaders, if we are being perfectly honest - approach their legacies driven by their egos, Marcus Aurelius begins instead with a foundation of gratitude.

Negative feelings are easier to default to, as they are often reflections of lessons that had very real and negative consequences. If you smell twelve flowers, and one of them results in a bee sting, you better believe you'll be remembering the flower resulting in the bee sting most vividly! But gratitude is often a conscious effort and an intentional moment where you take stock and appreciate what you have.

Even if the people in your life were not perfect people – and perhaps you were not perfect yourself – take a moment to appreciate what has been imparted to you from others. Valuable memories, practical skills, pieces of wisdom. If you were writing your own book of meditations that would tide you through your old age, what would you like to remember?

Follow my example, based off Marcus Aurelius' template, and take a moment to write your own down:

From my father I learned to question everything and hold steady to my beliefs. I learned to dedicate myself through persistence and hard work and to not do things by halves.

From my mother I learned to cultivate peace and diplomacy, and that the choices of others don't have to be my own. I learned a love of books and crafts and to express my creativity. She also taught me how to activate changes in my life, including spring cleaning binges accompanied by energetic music.

From my grandfather I learned humility and how to hold it in balance with integrity and quiet strength. From my nana I learned kindness and love, as well as how to knit and embroider. She taught me to love through crafts and how to show care to people even at a distance.

From my grandmother I learned a love of nature and grace towards humans. She taught me what it means to be generous of spirit and how to care for those with disabilities. She also taught me how to live life with a sense of humour as well as how to maintain boundaries when they are pushed.

From my brother I learned the meaning of pacifism in action and how to avoid being personally affected by other people's drama. He taught me how to draw back and look at both what was in my circle of control as well as what was within my circle of concern.

From my husband, I learned that is never too late to learn to ride a bike and that goals can be set and achieved at any age – but that it is also okay to abandon things that no longer serve their purpose, and pivoting is both acceptable and necessary.

From my daughter I have learned an appreciation of whimsical delights and that novel things that bring joy for a day can be just as valuable as things that last forever.

From my son I have learned that joy can come in unexpected places, and that sometimes making a new friend can be as easy as reaching out and asking.

If you have started a commonplace book. Or you have a scrapbook/photo album, compile your photos, memories and lessons together in one place.

Looking at yourself with a foundation of gratitude can help you identify the valuable traits you have which may be understated and otherwise fly under the radar. Seeing these parts of yourself and holding them with appreciation for a moment can help you become more self-aware and more in tune with who you are and where you have come from.

It can also assist with forgiving yourself for past mistakes. We often hold ourselves to unrealistic expectations, revisiting moments from the past and regretting our reactions as though we could have known the consequences before they happened - the burden of hindsight. But looking at ourselves with forgiveness, grace and gratitude can shift those moments of self-inflicted torture to calm acceptance:

I regret being taken in by that person's charisma and following their bad advice. With hindsight I can see that they didn't have my best interests at heart, and it was a naïve mistake to believe them and put so much weight on their words. But being able to recognize it now, I can see how I've grown as a person and I'm glad I possess the wisdom not to fall for the same mistake twice.

That regret has now been placed back into the past, forming its proper place in my own personal story arc of folly to wisdom. I no longer have to spend my time thinking about that regret and can instead fill my time with moments of appreciation.

Every time I do embroidery, for example, I think of my nana and the care and love she gave me when I was at her house during the school holidays. Some people swear by writing gratitude journals, either consciously like the Meditations example, or jotting down bullet points in a book once a day. Others may prefer to work gratitude into their day with conscious actions that bring positive thoughts to mind.

Ideas to bring gratitude into your present:

- Start a gratitude journal.
- Plant flowers that remind you of a person.
- Buy two mugs and send one to a loved one – every time you have a cup of tea you can think of that person and their impact on your life.
- Find a picture of a place associated with positive memories for you and print it out.
- Send a message to a person who had a big impact on you.
- Take some time to think about how far you have come and forgive yourself for your previous shortcomings.
- Treat yourself to something you will enjoy.

- Make yourself something delicious – a loved childhood snack, a cup of delicious tea or your favourite dinner.
- Take some time to appreciate the most important people in your life and do something nice for them.

Traditions

Traditions are something I've considered a lot over the years. Traditions can have both positive and negative associations depending on your relationship with them. They can provide structure, stability, a sense of national or cultural identity, and a sense of connectedness with your community. They can be a way of honouring the past and your personal history or be an excuse for a celebration. They can also be a source of stress and obligation or a tool for control that perpetuates negative influences in your life.

Thinking critically about the traditions you observe and deciding intentionally on what you would like to keep in your life could transform your personal and social landscape and help to cultivate the things you really value.

Growing up in a Christian family, the biggest traditions that marked the year for me were Christmas and Easter. Every Christmas we would go out of town and stay with our extended family, have a Christmas feast and a walk shortly afterwards. We would have Christmas stockings in the morning and open presents with the family together later that day – if we were lucky, someone would be convinced to drive us to the Boxing Day sales and we'd see what we could find for under $10. The period between Christmas and New Years would be frequented with walks along the beach by my nana's house, and plenty of unsupervised time where my brother and I would find crabs in the mudflats, build a colosseum out of sand and force them to fight until most of them were missing claws and the mightiest crab would be re-released as the victor. In hindsight, perhaps we could have done with more supervision.

Easter would often involve gorging on chocolate, including one special Easter bunny each and sleeping in tents at church camp.

Those memories are strong because they're tied together with food and are revisited every year.

Family rituals and shared experiences form a sense of nostalgia, which can strengthen family bonds and a sense of belonging. This can be a really positive thing, although it can of course turn sour if your family is toxic and you should really be *disconnecting* from them rather than reconnecting. The stress and obligation around family traditions and the associated expectations can be incredibly stifling and aggravating. It's no coincidence that reports of domestic violence spike every year around Christmas and New Years.

Throughout my adulthood and as I've stepped into parenthood, I've met many other parents who have put effort into making their own family traditions. Much like other periods in history which have seen mass migration, the present age sees many people move around and away from their families for a multitude of reasons. Modern education and awareness of trauma is one, as people step out into their own lives and out of the shadow of their history. The inability to buy a home due to economic instability is another, as people shift from rental to rental and seek out places where they can afford to live comfortably. Work opportunities and the accessibility of travel is another, which sees people starting fresh in new cities or countries as they reach out to break new ground. Whatever the reason, it can form a sense of disconnectedness if your old traditions no longer fit, and looking for new ways to observe them – or new traditions altogether, may help you feel more grounded in your life.

In New Zealand, my demographic is often described on paperwork as 'NZ European' as my ancestors came from a variety of European countries: Scotland, England, Ireland, Denmark and the Czech Republic being the most prominent. Very few traditions – other than the Christian holiday observations – have remained in my family, and my demographic by nature points me to a feeling of otherness and displacement. The other word I can use to describe myself is *'Pākehā'* – a Māori word for non-Māori, which some people feel uncomfortable with as it uses an *'other'* language to describe themselves which doesn't particularly help with the feeling of *'otherness'*. For me, however, it lends something that 'NZ European' doesn't, as it has an attachment to the land I was born on, and the people who initially welcomed my ancestors (pre-land wars), and the integration and relationship my family has had with Māori for generations.

Considering your place within your community can

help you find your place within your world and lay down roots – even if at times you feel like an apple tree in a grove of kauri or oaks.

Learning your own history, and the history of the places that you come from can also help you connect with yourself and form your identity. History is full of good, bad and neutral influences and it's up to you to decide which things you would like to carry forwards into the future and how you would like to experience them.

On 24 June 2022 Aotearoa New Zealand celebrated Matariki as an official public holiday for the first time. Matariki is Māori New Year, celebrated when the Matariki constellation (also known as the Pleiades) rises for the first time each year. This signals a time to come together, honour the dead, celebrate the present, and plan for the future. While this tradition has been kept alive all along by Māori and Pasifika people, its inclusion as a public holiday has opened the door for all New Zealanders to learn how to celebrate Matariki and build new family rituals and traditions around it.

Our own family attends council driven events and the local events held by the school. When my children went to kindergarten/preschool, families would bring along a vegetable to cook up into a large soup and everyone would go stargazing together in the early evening. At primary school, the school would put on a display for Matariki artwork and songs for the extended family to come and see, and the parents' association would host food and drink afterwards. While I never grew up with Matariki, my children will have strong memories around it.

I know other families who every year buy new pyjamas for New Year and stay up to watch movies. I know another woman who since splitting from her family and becoming a Christian spends time on Christmas by herself with a loaf of Turkish bread and a glass of wine, marinating herself in the feeling of being loved and appreciated – I mistook her for lonely and invited her out when I first heard of this ritual, but she explained it was something positive and personal she did as it helped her reconnect with herself and God.

I know another woman who around Matariki every year sits down to plan her entire year of planting, taking stock of seeds and ordering what she needs. This places her not only on her land, but within the seasons of the year and within her family as she calculates how much she will need to feed them all.

Another community I lived in for a while had an unofficial preserving day, where people would bring produce and preserve jars of food, working together and reaping the rewards.

Traditions and rituals can be things you do personally for yourself, they can be for your family – nuclear and/or extended, and they can be within your wider social circles – your friends or your entire community. They might look strange to others, or they might feel strange to you as you consider new things to try. Perhaps you feel divorced from your culture and want to reconnect with it - you could have a look at your own personal heritage and think of ways to experience it in a fresh way. Traditions and rituals when it comes down to it, are a way of finding and practicing meaning within your own context.

Consider the traditions you observed as a child. What did they mean to you? Do you have any strong memories, or a sense of nostalgia? Are there any things you would like to bring forward? If there are negative connotations, are there things that you would like to leave behind? Keeping your end goal in mind, what feelings would you like to cultivate and is there anything you would like to feel more connected with?

Have a look through the following list and consider if there is anything you would like to celebrate or learn more about? Make a note of it and spend some time looking into it further to decide how you would like to experience it.

Annual traditions:

- Your birthday
- New Year celebrations
- Days of religious observance
- Christmas and adjacent observations (Christmas, Yule & Winter Solstice, Festivus etc)
- Days of national observance (July 4th, Bastille Day, ANZAC Day etc)
- Days of cultural observance (Burns Night, St Patrick's Day, Matariki, Diwali, etc)
- Random Act of Kindness Day
- Women's History Month
- Black History Month
- Banned Book Month
- April Fool's Day
- Star Wars Day – May 4th
- International Tea Day – May 21st

- Pink Shirt Day
- Hobbit Day – Sept 22nd

Regular traditions:

- Beginning and end of each season
- Regular get-togethers for boardgames, books or sharing food
- Attending school or community events
- Planting days
- Deep cleaning days
- Family movie night
- Date night

Ways you might like to celebrate:

Themed dinners – invite friends, pick dishes to contribute, make a playlist and dress up! Fantasy tavern or regency tea party, pick what appeals to you and your friends.

Hygge gathering – have some cozy snacks and company by the fireside with fairy lights for mood lighting.

Book club – find other bibliophiles and share your latest reads. Pick one together and dress up as characters or swap books off your backlist and have some chill conversations.

Gift exchange – sharing baking recipes, DIY gifts, misc finds from thrift shops or personal presents bought with the person in mind – setting a theme or challenge can be fun, as well as setting up a gift exchange network within your social circle to keep things within budget.

Clothes Swap – empty out your wardrobe of things that no longer fit and set up a night to trade clothes with friends. It's like a Tupperware Party where no one has to actually spend any money!

Spring Cleaning – getting your home into a state where you can enjoy it and refreshing all your decorations for a fresh start.

Dungeons and Dragons – or other RPG/board games – get a group together and commit to a campaign for an ongoing game. Pandemic Legacies and Dungeons and Dragons have been fantastic experiences for me, and great ways to meet new people.

Pub Quiz Night – are there any pubs or taverns in your vicinity which host quiz nights? Get a group together and put your collective knowledge to the test.

Art classes – sip and paint or live drawings, this could shift from learning a new skill to adopting a new lifestyle! Are there any kinds of artwork you'd like to learn? You don't need to keep to acrylics if something else tickles your fancy – pottery? Photography? Movie making? Have a look at what is available in your area.

Skillshare evening – get together with friends and teach each other your skills. You'll be surprised at what you can learn from each other and will make deep connections at the same time.

Stitch 'N' Bitch – gather your craft-loving friends and making things together while catching up on the latest gossip.

Board Games

Board games provide a cozy atmosphere and the opportunity for genuine connections. Many libraries also now provide board games as well as books – and if yours doesn't, it's not unreasonable to ask them to start!

Inviting friends over for board games or meeting new people at public board game events are a great way to enjoy real connections with people. Even in the Jane Austen era, people often came together to play rounds of whist or other card games. Try some old favourites or branch out and learn something new!

In a 2019 review of recent studies and literature on board games and their benefits by the National

Library of Medicine, board games have been found to be a beneficial tool for promoting good physical and mental health. In one long term study, the risk of dementia was measured as 15% lower in participants who played board games. Other studies have found board games to help with anxiety, ADHD, and Alzheimer's. Board games have also been found to help people overcoming addictions such as smoking.[33]

While I'm sure everyone knows the classic games like Monopoly, Scrabble and Ticket to Ride, there is a huge world full of board games from smaller publishers that are both readily available and a lot of fun! Boardgamegeek.com provides comprehensive reviews of thousands of board games, including complexity levels, average play times and the ability to sort by category.

Take a moment to put a wish list together of games that suit your personality – do you prefer competitive or collaborative? Fast paced or cozy? Two-player, large group games or single player?

Here are a few recommendations from my board

---

[33] https://www.ncbi.nlm.nih.gov/pmc/articles/PMC6380050/

game shelf:

Patchwork

2 Player

In this cozy abstract drafting game, two players progress around the central board and collect Tetris-style patchwork pieces to complete their quilt! As you use your own personal grid board to complete your quilt, this fast-paced game is satisfying and strategic without too much room for mean-spiritedness.

Jaipur

2 Player

With beautiful tokens and game-pieces, Jaipur is both competitive and cozy. This two-player game sees players buying, selling and trading through a combination of strategy and luck to see who will become the most powerful merchant!

Wingspan

1-5 Players

Beautifully illustrated by Beth Sobel with over 170 individual bird cards in the base deck, this game is a pleasure to play. Collect birds in each of your habitats, lay eggs and gain food tokens from a 3D bird-house themed dice tower. Each person has their own player mat, giving them full control over their own habitats. This game also features automa rules for those who love playing single-player! With several expansions now available, this board game provides endless fun and has a dedicated fanbase.

Calico
1-4 Players
Also illustrated by Beth Sobel, this gorgeous tile-laying game sets you the challenge of creating a quilt and form patterns to attract cats and place buttons to score points.

Cascadia
1-4 Players
This gorgeous tile-laying game features Beth Sobel's beautiful illustrations and challenges players to build the most harmonious habitat with hexagonal terrain tiles and wildlife tokens. Bonus points are scored for forming specific animal patterns and wildlife corridors. Using habitats and wildlife of the Pacific Northwest, tokens feature foxes, salmon, elk, bears and hawks.

Marrying Mr. Darcy
2-6 Players
This role-playing card game invites players to dive into Pride and Prejudice as different bachelorettes competing for courtship of their ideal suitors.

Everdell

1-4 Players

Set in the valley of Everdell, populated by adorable creatures, this worker placement game has a gorgeous vibe as well as beautiful artwork and game pieces. A large three-dimensional tree is the centerpiece of the game as you work through seasons deciding how to build your town to score the most points. With a single player mode available, this game is a wonderful escapist dream.

Azul

2-4 Players

This award-winning game uses gorgeous tiles inspired by the interior of the Alhambra. In this game, you are a tile-laying artist drawing and laying tiles to decorate the interior of the Royal Palace of Evora! Points are scored for each tile laid, specific patterns that have been accomplished and points deducted for wasted supplies. This game is competitive, beautiful and overall satisfying.

No Thanks!

3-5 Players / 3-7 Players (2011 edition)

This fast-paced game has simple rules and is easy to pick up, but is engaging, competitive and perfect for small parties with an estimated game time of around 20 minutes. Players choose to pick up cards or use chips from their personal supply to skip to the next player. This game balances luck and audacity as players try to bluff and gamble their way to the lowest score.

Tokaido

2-5 Players

Tokaido sets players on a scenic adventure across the East Sea Road of Japan, as they use their resources to eat food, buy souvenirs, visit temples and collect panorama cards. Whether you win or lose, this game is a peaceful escape and a delight to play.

Arboretum

2-4 Players

Another game featuring Beth Sobel's art, this strategy card game sees you laying down patterns of beautiful trees to design your own arboretum. A little complex to score but a pleasure to play, with multiple strategies to win.

Sushi Go

2-5 Players

A super-fast card game that is incredibly easy to pick up, this is a great one to play with the kids. Players are dining at a sushi restaurant and aim to snatch up dishes before they pass by, building sets to score points.

The Fox in the Forest

2 Players

This fairy-tale based card game involves taking tricks to score points with beautiful cards featuring different powers. This edition is competitive, while Fox in the Forest Duet is the collaborative version with players working together to defeat the game.

My Shelfie

2-4 Players

This beautiful abstract game sees players drafting tiles to fill their three-dimensional bookshelf in a game that resembles a combination of interior design and Connect 4. Bonus points are scored if you can complete patterns on your personal challenge card.

Books

What better way to create a cozy escapist dream than to fill your home with beautiful books that can sweep you away to exciting destinations from the safety of your armchair? Having more books than you can possibly read in your lifetime in your home is a great way to ensure you'll never be bored.

Studies have found that reading has multiple benefits, from cognitive engagement related to vocabulary, reasoning, concentration and critical thinking to soft skills including empathy, social perception, and emotional intelligence. They have also found that compared to reading magazines and newspapers, study participants who read at least a chapter a day had lower mortality rates – so reading could yet save your life![34]

If you still need convincing, lining your outer walls with bookshelves can increase your home insulation and help you keep warm and toasty without blowing your energy budget. You officially have permission – go buy more books!

If you find yourself in a reading slump, try changing genres and going for a light read. Reading romance books with a happily-ever-after guarantee, or young adult fiction which tends to have lighter vocabulary, shorter sentences and a faster pace can help you get back into the habit of reading if it has been a while. Listening to audiobooks also counts, and you can most likely access a huge number for free with your library card.

Expand your personal library:

- Trawl through your local op shops and see what bargains you can find
- Seek out your favourite childhood books and put a nostalgic collection together
- Collect different editions of your favourite book (can you ever have too many copies of

---

[34] https://www.ncbi.nlm.nih.gov/pmc/articles/PMC5105607/

Pride and Prejudice?)
- Set up a wishlist of books on Amazon
- Ask friends what their favourite books are and buy or borrow a copy
- Check out your local bookshop for bargains and new releases
- Arrange yourself a cozy book nook, cook up some reading snacks, unplug the wifi and turn off your phone for some dedicated reading time!

I've collected a list of books that have a cottagecore vibe below and sorted them into categories by interest.

Classic Books:

The Anne of Green Gables series by L. M. Montgomery:

- Anne of Green Gables (1908)
- Anne of Avonlea (1909)
- Anne of the Island (1915)
- Anne of Windy Poplars (1936)
- Anne's House of Dreams (1917)
- Anne of Ingleside (1939)
- Rainbow Valley (1919)
- Rilla of Ingleside (1921)

The works of Jane Austen:

- Sense and Sensibility (1811)
- Pride and Prejudice (1813)
- Mansfield Park (1814)
- Emma (1815)
- Northanger Abbey (1818)
- Persuasion (1818)
- Lady Susan (1871)

The works of the Brontë sisters:

Charlotte Brontë:

- Jane Eyre (1847)
- Shirley (1849)
- Vilette (1853)
- The Professor (1857)

Emily Brontë:

- Wuthering Heights (1847)

Anne Brontë:

- Agnes Grey (1847)
- The Tenant of Wildfell Hall (1848)

Selected works by George Eliot:

- The Mill on the Floss (1860)
- Silas Marner (1861)

- Middlemarch (1871-72)

Little Women series by Louisa May Alcott:

- Little Women (1868)
- Good Wives (1869)
- Little Men (1871)
- Jo's Boys (1886)

Selected works of Francess Hodgson Burnett:

- Little Lord Fauntleroy (1886)
- A Little Princess (1905)
- The Secret Garden (1911)

Little House on the Prairie series by Laura Ingalls Wilder:

- Little House in the Big Woods (1932)
- Farmer Boy (1933)
- Little House on the Prairie (1935)
- On the Banks of Plum Creek (1937)
- By the Shores of Silver Lake (1939)
- The Long Winter (1940)
- Little Town on the Prairie (1941)
- These Happy golden Years (1943)
- The First Four Years (1971)

The Borrowers series by Mary Norton:

- The Borrowers (1952)

- The Borrowers Afield (1955)
- The Borrowers Afloat (1959)
- The Borrowers Aloft (1961)
- Poor Stainless (1966)
- The Borrowers Avenged (1982)

The Chronicles of Narnia series by C. S. Lewis:

- The Lion, the Witch and the Wardrobe (1950)
- Prince Caspian: The Return to Narnia (1951)
- The Voyage of the Dawn Treader (1952)
- The Silver Chair (1953)
- The Horse and His Boy (1954)
- The Magician's Nephew (1955)
- The Last Battle (1956)

Howl's Moving Castle series by Diana Wynne Jones:

- Howl's Moving Castle (1986)
- House of Many Ways (2008)
- Castle in the Air (1990)

Other classics:

- The Hobbit by J. R. R. Tolkein (1935)
- Tuck Everlasting by Natalie Babbitt (1975)
- Heidi by Johanna Spyri (1880)
- Swallows and amazons by Arthur Ransome (1930)

Recent Cozy Books:

Legends and Lattes by Travis Baldree (2022)

Emily Wilde's Encyclopaedia of Faeries by Heather Fawcett (2023)

You Can't Spell Treason Without Tea by Rebecca Thorne (2022)

The Tea Dragon Society by Kay O'Neill (2017)

The Honey Witch by Sydney J. Shields (2024)

The House Witch by Delemhach (2024)

The Hedge Witch by Cari Thomas (2022)

The Wandering Inn by Pirateaba
(available to read online for free at thewanderinginn.com)

The House in the Cerulean Sea by T. J. Klune (2020)

Flowerheart by Catherine Bakewell (2023)

The Very Secret Society of Irregular Witches by Sangu Mandanna (2022)

The Bee Man's Husband by Laura Wolf (2023)

Maud by Laura Wolf (2023)

The Jane Austen Society by Natalie Jenner (2020)

Chai Time and Cinnamon Gardens by Shankari Chandran (2023)

Nonfiction Books:

At Home: A Short History of Private Life by Bill Bryson (2010)

The Subversive Stitch: Embroidery and the Making of the Feminine by Roszika Parker (1984)

The Fabric of Civilization: How Textiles Made the World by Virginia Postrel (2020)

Threads of Life: A History of the World Through the Eye of a Needle by Clare Hunter (2020)

If Walls Could Talk: An Intimate History of the Home by Lucy Worsley (2012)

Jane Austen at Home by Lucy Worsley (2017)

Meik Wiking's Books:

- The Little Book of Hygge (2016)
- The Little Book of Lykke (2017)
- The Art of Making Memories (2019)
- The Key to Happiness (2019)
- My Hygge Home (2022)
- The Art of Danish Living (2024)

Lagom: The Swedish Art of Balanced Living by Linnea Dunne (2017)

The Little Book of Fika by Lynda Balslev (2018)

American Cozy: Hygge-Inspired Ways to Create Comfort and Happiness by Stephanie Pederson (2018)

Games

Stardew Valley

A popular farming sim game with a cult following – and for a good reason! Developed by Eric Barone aka ConcernedApe, Stardew Valley introduces you to Pelican Town, where you inherit your grandfather's farm, battle monsters in the mine and interact with the townsfolk – some of whom are candidates for marriage. Stardew Valley is also a one-time purchase game, with Eric Barone stating he will never charge for DLC content – which is a rare and much appreciated stance in the age of micro-transactions. Eric's next project, which is currently in development, is the much-anticipated Haunted Chocolatier. Stardew Valley also has a delightful board game, cookbook and cross stitch book available on the merch store.

Be warned that Stardew Valley does contain adult themes in some of the NPC's stories and may not be suitable for young children.

Animal Crossing

A mainstream social simulation game, where you interact with anthropomorphic animal villagers, collect and sell resources and customize your environment.

Tiny Glade

A fairly new release with extremely high user ratings, Tiny Glade is a sandbox diorama building game with simple controls and enchanting visuals.

A Short Hike

A cute exploration game where your character is tasked with reaching the summit of the mountain to get cellphone reception – and filled with interactions, distractions and little surprises along the way. You won't be able to help meandering and taking your time to get to your destination.

Potion Craft

An alchemy simulator where you gather ingredients, solve puzzles and brew potions for customers who enter your shop. Whether you brew nice potions to heal the sick or dreadful potions to assist in theft and murder affects your karma and what kind of customers will be attracted to your store.

Paleo Pines

An adorable village simulation game which combines collecting dinosaurs, farming resources and interacting with townsfolk.

Palia

Palia is an online multiplayer open world cozy RPG game where you explore, garden, hunt, catch bugs, craft objects and decorate your home. A great place to meet up with friends or make new ones.

Kingdom Come: Deliverance

An action RPG game in an immersive medieval setting, this game is full of quests as well as historically accurate details in an open world, letting you explore not just the plot but amazing details of architecture and textile design. The stained-glass windows and tapestries are an absolute highlight of this game.

Adjacent Aesthetics

Cottagecore is one of many aesthetic trends in the ever-changing landscape of social media algorithms. While we've journeyed deep into the history and philosophies of cottagecore, you might find it isn't quite for you – but there are plenty further rabbit holes for you to plumb the depths of, and there will be plenty more that will come into being after the publication of this book. These are a few of the other aesthetics and microtrends that border cottagecore:

Cluttercore

Drawing inspiration from places like thrift shops and Studio Ghibli films, cluttercore appreciates the objects people find joy in and celebrates the chaos of creativity and collecting.

Ravencore/Crowcore

The ravencore trend is a little darker in nature to cottagecore, taking pleasure in gothic and morbid things with a natural bend such as animal skulls, feathers, and shiny things like metals or gems and crystals. Ravencore takes inspiration from the nature of the birds themselves as well as poetry such as *The Raven* by Edgar Allan Poe.

Goblincore

Goblincore has been described as cottagecore's dirty cousin, taking pleasure in the 'ugly' and things that are not traditionally accepted as beautiful. Frogs, toads, mushrooms, toadstools and snails are mainstays of the goblincore aesthetic. Goblincore has also found appreciation from the LGBTQ+ community, and those who like to build their own definitions of beauty. Goblincore and ravencore/crowcore have a lot of crossover, but goblincore can tend towards the magical end of the spectrum where ravencore edges towards the natural world.

Fairycore

Fairycore centres around the idea of the fey or fairy folk and can be presented as a genuine belief in the fey, an appreciation of folklore or an embracing of the fashion including dressing or cosplaying as fey.

The natural world, particularly flowers and flower garlands are popular in this aesthetic, as well as a shift from the home into the outdoors.

Light Academia

The academia aesthetics centre around books and bookshelves, with light academia embracing light colours and content. Light coloured wood, natural tones, and plenty of natural light in a home library form an ideal light academia vibe. The cheerful bookshop in Disney's Beauty and the Beast featuring Belle swinging by on a rolling bookshelf-ladder is likely one of the early triggers many people felt that directed them towards this aesthetic.

Dark Academia

Dark academia is similarly based around a love of books and the literary word but tends towards darker woods and leather bound tomes with a more serious vibe. Bram Stoker's Dracula and some dark-tinted bottles that look like they would belong in a dingy apothecary would not be amiss in a dark academia home-library.

Barbiecore

Barbiecore is a hyper-feminist trend that embraces wearing pink and celebrating women. With many people dressing up to attend the 2023 Barbie movie and the Barbie-box photo booths that populated cinemas as well as theme-parties, this trend skyrocketed almost overnight as people shared their looks. The revival in Barbie-love has seen a social media trend that has long out-lived the screening of the movie with self-portrait posts proclaiming "This Barbie *insert achievement here*" as individuals reclaim their voices of self-confidence. The Barbiecore aesthetic is characterized by an overwhelming amount of pink and a love of accessories.

Mermaidcore

To a lesser extent than Barbie, but no less important to those who love this aesthetic, The Little Mermaid movie of 2023 prompted a revival of the love of all things mermaid. Mermaidcore has a more natural bend than Barbiecore, favouring a beach palette and an appreciation of natural materials such as shells and coral. Mermaidcore, like cottagecore, brings you closer to nature but bridges the paradoxical gap between two worlds. Mermaidcore fashion incorporates lace, silk, tulle, mesh and sequins.

Balletcore

Balletcore obviously draws inspiration from ballet dancers and ballet culture, and is styled after a combination of athleticism, art and beautiful tulle skirts. Balletcore loves to embrace hardwood floors and natural surfaces and infuses elegance and dance into every part of life.

Balletcore influencers are seen in their videos incorporating dance and rhythm into every part of their lives from crossing the road to picking toys off the floor. This blurring of lines between recreation and the rest of life can be seen as both commentary on the lack of time people – particularly women – have allocated to recreation in modern life, as well as a stubborn resistance towards letting go of the beautiful things and passions that bring joy to life as we age.

Coquette

The coquette trend embraces the hyper-feminine soft-girl aesthetic, drawing inspiration from Victorian and Rococo fashion with modern romantic twists like Bridgerton. Coquette fashion includes soft pastels, soft and warm shades of white, natural lighting and make-up, babydoll dresses, blouses, corsets, dainty lace stockings, bows and often a lot of skin with natural tan-lines.

Coquette trends bring to mind the muses of artists in their use of casual luxury and the natural form. It defaults towards more flirtatious content than cottagecore, and at times borders Lolita fashion and themes.

Blokette

Blokette is the gen-Z adaptation of the 90s tomboy trend, and a reaction to coquette, with a rejection of the hyper-feminine in favour of practical and comfortable clothing – often blending women's and men's clothing and wearing vintage sportswear in a more 'girly' and feminine fashion. A blokette outfit, for example, might pair an adidas track jacket with a frilly skirt and either walking shoes or ballet flats. Blokette, while not as widespread as some of the other aesthetics, is a great example of how trends and aesthetics splinter and react to each other according to the needs of expression and philosophy. While cottagecore seems to be more long-lasting than many of its smaller neighbours, the blokette trend gives voice to the need to say "I can be both sporty and girly."

The Dark Side of Cottagecore

Feeling inspired and wanting to start a cottagecore channel of your own?

I'd advise you to pause before you take the plunge, as there is a surprising amount of toxicity associated with a hashtag that seems bright, cheerful and carefree. With the way the internet works, you can start out watching videos on how to tie hair ribbons or plant a butterfly garden and before you know it, you're knee-deep in consumerism, white supremacy or patriarchal propaganda. Cottagecore hashtags have been adopted by a lot of bad actors using the term to net views for nefarious purposes.

The cottagecore movement has gone through a lot of rapid changes over the last several years, and for deep and complex reasons that are intertwined with history, politics and ideology. If you are considering creating content for the cottagecore community or getting involved in online social forums, it is important to know what you're getting into as the aesthetic attracts people for very different and at times concerning reasons and these people may be lurking in the comments section without your knowledge.

In its early days, cottagecore found popularity with the sapphic and queer community on Tumblr, and it is easy to see why. The cozy and feminine themes are the same vibes you get with virally popular sapphic romantasy books like Legends and Lattes – they're safe places filled with feminine beauty and low stakes activities like picking berries, dancing, and baking bread.

One of the big problems with this idyllic aesthetic is that the ideals and beauty standards of femininity can be very narrow and with #cottagecore rising in popularity, the algorithms pushed creators that met those beauty standards to the forefront of social media feeds – bolstered by celebrity influencers who could pay their way to the front of the line. This has, in many newsfeeds, narrowed the representation of what cottagecore is to blonde, Caucasian women with small waists, perfect make-up and expensive kitchens.

Many of the celebrity influencers have also been critiqued for their inauthenticity and share some similarities with Marie Antoinette as she was accused of cosplaying rustic poverty during a time when there was a very real wealth gap. The very concept of a fully cottagecore life is unattainable except for the very rich – the Marie Antoinettes and the celebrity influencers – the rest of us can only achieve small things when and where we can around our work, whether it is in or out of the home.

Due to the popularity cottagecore found online, it also became a frequently used search term for clothing, and Google search results will direct shoppers to fast-fashion brands like Temu, Shein, or Amazon. While the early cottagecore movement valued quality hand-made and tailored clothing, internet traffic now pushes people to low-quality bulk made dresses inspired from the original posts through the magic of marketing.

Internet traffic driven by profit and production directs people seeking the escapism of cottagecore further into the vortex that created the world we want to escape from. We now have decisions to make about buying fast-fashion clothes – some of which come from dubious sources laced with accusations of plagiarizing designs, exploitative labour practices and suspicion of containing hazardous chemicals well beyond recommended limits – or shelling out hundreds of dollars to get custom made clothing to match the images we see celebrities wearing. Or, of course, making our own clothes which comes with costs and challenges of its own. To put it broadly, there are a lot of extra complications to think about when all you are really seeking is simplicity and peace, which makes an unattainable life feel even more out of reach.

In this vein, there are two main online communities which encroach upon the cottagecore aesthetic from different but related angles: homesteading and tradwife. Both of these trends contain a lot of inspirational and positive content which have brought people joy, but also have inherent problematic elements that complicate the cottagecore dream.

The tradwife (or traditional wife) movement shares a lot of commonalities with cottagecore ideals – it looks selectively for inspiration in a rose-tinted version of the past, but it creates a hyper-feminine ideal to adhere to which is controversial at least and extremely damaging at worst.

A 'tradwife' in its most simple definition is a woman who believes and practices what they believe to be traditional gender roles within a marriage context. "Traditional" can of course refer to a huge variety of ideas depending on religious ideas, cultural practices and values, and individual interpretations of what all of this means to them. Some people use the term somewhat innocently, while others have specific agendas related to their ideology.

There is nothing wrong with holding traditional values or participating in traditional gender roles. There is a lot wrong, however, with misrepresenting traditional roles, cultures and philosophies out of a place of ignorance or exploitation, and there is also a lot wrong with holding others to a standard or ideals that they do not wish to be held to.

When people look to a culture that is not their own for inspiration and try to adopt elements of what they believe that life looks like, it can sometimes be considered cultural appropriation, especially if it is done in bad faith or without respect. The culture under the microscope is butchered, cherry picking parts of who they are and ignoring others, giving an incomplete and often stereotyped view that can be deeply insulting.

The tone of this differs noticeably from creators who look to reconnect with their own heritage or for understanding and engagement with other cultures in a respectful way. A fantastic example of respectful exploration is historical costumer @VBirchwood on YouTube.

The tradwife movement is also heavily informed by the 1950s image of a housewife and The American Dream, the anti-work movement, conservative Christian family values, and has been heavily promoted by the alt-right and hypermasculine communities which find a home for their extreme ideologies online. In January 2024, Forbes investigated the psychological harms that the tradwife movement has towards women and children, and the connections it has with white supremacy.[35] The article explains that extremist politics are blended seamlessly and strategically through posts with aesthetics of femininity, beauty

---

[35] https://www.forbes.com/sites/traversmark/2024/01/06/a-psychologist-explains-the-dangers-of-the-tradwife-movement/

and relationships which are used as a tool for promoting anti-feminist messages. While being a tradwife is promoted as an empowering choice, the reality of what they are promoting is a disempowerment of women tied up in unrealistic and rigid expectations alongside an erosion of self-esteem when the ideals are not met.

An awareness of where these particular pictures of femininity are drawn from and the darker underbelly that accompanies them is important for keeping one foot on the ground. Escapism can be good for a while, but if the place you're escaping to is a cage, you should know it before shutting the door behind you.

The 1950s American Housewife ideal as it is marketed, valued the housewife as a valid career and full-time role. When many people are feeling underappreciated at work or are fearful of the idea of not spending enough time with their kids, it's an attractive lifestyle. For many people it is the reality of their life. I, myself, am also a stay-at-home mother and an author and artist on the side. It's great. But the picture that the 1950s image presents comes alongside disempowerment. It comes with an infantilization of women as less capable of intelligent or physical tasks and places them directly and exclusively within the feminine sphere. It places the burden of domestic and emotional labour squarely on their shoulders and places them in a submissive role under their husbands. This then leads to situations where women can feel trapped and lose the ability to choose. To ignore this reality is a disservice to those who find themselves, through folly or circumstance, back within this reality with no visible way out.

Figure 15 Alcoa Aluminum Advert.

Unfortunately, a lot of the critiques I have seen lack empathy and understanding of the people they claim to be defending. I've seen this recently with responses to a tradwife channel that went through the rounds on TikTok. People were concerned that the tradwife in question was being exploited by her husband – however, the preoccupations some of the critics had showed they had little empathy with her actual life or situation.

"She has nine children! Nine children! Nine!" one TikToker repeated. She had little appreciation for the fact that some people *do* want that many children. While women have definitely been pressured or forced into having children, which is by all means totally unacceptable, some people do legitimately want to have large families and that is just as valid a choice as those who choose to remain child-free.

The hyper-femininity associated with tradwives can be a stifling and restrictive definition of what it means to be feminine, but the critical response to it runs the risk of doing just the same. Unfortunately, the algorithms employed by social media thrive on outrage and some of the most polarizing content can easily rise to the top.

Streams of thought from the problematic past still persist today and some of the people attracted to aesthetics such as cottagecore are attracted to it for all the wrong reasons. Rigid gender roles and particularly ideals that require women to be submissive to be feminine are extremely dangerous and concerning. "Wife training" and "behavioral correction" is a toxic concept that accompanies tradwife content and makes light of domestic abuse as an acceptable or even positive thing. An article in a 1964 edition of Time Magazine explained the 'helpful overtones' of a man beating his wife as a "temporary therapy" for men:

"The periods of violent behavior by the husband," the doctors observed, "served to release him momentarily from his anxiety about his ineffectiveness as a man, while giving his wife apparent masochistic gratification and helping probably to deal with the guilt arising from the intense hostility expressed in her controlling, castrating behavior."[36]

While it would be comfortable to believe these views are confined to the 1960s, they've found purchase in the "manosphere", and "alpha male" circles online led by influences like Andrew Tate.

Quotes circulating the internet attributed to Andrew Tate include:

"Women need to be protected from their own irrational impulses. They require guidance and discipline from men to keep them in line."

---

[36] https://time.com/archive/6813927/psychiatry-the-wife-beater-his-wife/

"Women are more emotional and less rational than men, which makes them unsuitable for leadership roles."

"Women are happiest when they are fulfilling their traditional roles as wives and mothers."

"A woman's value is directly proportional to her beauty and femininity."

"A woman's loyalty is only as strong as her options."[37]

It's important to remember that these issues are complex, especially for the vulnerable people living the reality. There can be a lot of push and pull factors that put people into disempowered situations, and many people are also born into environments which take extra-ordinary levels of bravery and/or desperation to leave. So, while the tradwife movement and disingenuous influencer channels do require a critical eye, making montages of their family videos highlighting pictures where they look particularly tired might, therefore, not be the most supportive response to someone you believe is in danger.

---

[37] https://medium.com//andrew-tate-quotes-about-women-1ca6470132be

According to the National Library of Medicine, domestic abuse affects as many as 1 in 4 women in the USA and 1 in 9 men.[38] Domestic abuse includes physical, sexual, economic, emotional, and psychological abuse and can be difficult to identify as it is not always reported to authorities and many leave it too late for complex reasons often involving shame, guilt and low self-esteem. Toleration and forgiveness of abuse often leads to increasing intensity of abuse so it is important if you find yourself in unsafe situations to extricate yourself as soon as possible and ask for help if you don't think you can do it alone.

NHI statistics show that of female homicide victims, 44% had previously visited a hospital emergency department within 2 years of their murder.[39] A study has also found that non-fatal strangulation is the highest predictor of murder, with 43% of participants experiencing strangulation before their murder. If you have been strangled even once by your partner, your risk of becoming a victim of homicide is increased by over 600%.[40]

---

[38] https://www.ncbi.nlm.nih.gov/books/NBK499891/
[39] Ibid.
[40] https://www.ncbi.nlm.nih.gov/pmc/articles/PMC2573025/

Figure 16 A Chase & Sanborn ad from 1952 making light of domestic violence.

It is also of note that searching for #tradwife content online will also direct you to the BDSM community, particularly the sub/dom subsect. A submissive-dominant or sub-dom relationship or role-playing involves the relinquishing of control from the submissive to the dominant person. There are complex and nuanced reasons why a person may want to engage in this kind of relationship, and it is not necessarily abuse – with the key difference being consent and freedom of choice. Consent is also a complex concept that many people do not have a good understanding of and may not necessarily know they are being abused. The Training Institute on Strangulation Prevention offers courses and resources on topics including the myth of consent for strangulation during intimacy.[41]

Even if you agree to something in advance, and even if you enjoyed it, it can still be non-consensual. Consent can be revoked and if you are not in a position where you can communicate that, you are in an unsafe environment.

If you agreed to something you did not want to do due to feeling unsafe or as though there will be a negative outcome if you do not comply, this can be a form of coercive control.

If you feel as though you need to comply or submit due to internalized shame surrounding religious

---

[41] https://www.strangulationtraininginstitute.com/

virtue or because it is God's will, this may be spiritual coercion and/or spiritual abuse.

If you are uncomfortable with the situation you find yourself in, it is worth seeking a second opinion – and potentially from someone outside of your community who can remain impartial.

The conservative Christian community also has a fair bit to answer for with persistent ideologies on femininity based on terrible theological practices that need to be challenged. The literal interpretation of Proverbs 31 as a yardstick for women is a perfect example.

One of my friends from Bible College described a dreadful first (and only) date she had when she was eighteen with a boy she'd been set up with from church. He drove to her house to pick her up, and once she took a seat and closed the door, he handed her a bible open to Proverbs 31.

"This is what I expect from you," he told her. "If you don't think you can meet this standard, you should get out now."

When looking at how to interpret Proverbs 31, it's important to understand the context of the original writing. It is not, in fact, a bullet-point checklist for wife shopping. It is an acrostic poem in its original language and is a form of ancient wisdom literature, using the concept of wisdom personified as a woman. A common misapplication of biblical verses stems from the belief that the Bible is an infallible document which leads to arrogant individuals blind to their own very fallible faculties interpreting translated texts without appreciation or understanding of where they come from, what they are or what they truly mean. Poetry when translated, for one thing, loses its form and structure. An acrostic poem in one language no longer looks like an acrostic poem in another. A chiastic structure when translated loses its shape and clarity. Wisdom literature misapplied becomes a pitfall of folly.

An excerpt from Proverbs 31 is copied below in the World English Bible translation, as it is one of the few translations in the public domain. I challenge you to read it keeping in mind the type of literature it is intended to be as well as the experience of a sheltered and inexperienced teenager being told this is what was literally expected of her:

PROVERBS 31

The words of King Lemuel—the revelation which his mother taught him:
"Oh, my son!
Oh, son of my womb!
Oh, son of my vows!
Don't give your strength to women,
nor your ways to that which destroys kings.
It is not for kings, Lemuel,
it is not for kings to drink wine,
nor for princes to say, 'Where is strong drink?'
lest they drink, and forget the law,
and pervert the justice due to anyone who is afflicted.
Give strong drink to him who is ready to perish,
and wine to the bitter in soul.
Let him drink, and forget his poverty,
and remember his misery no more.
Open your mouth for the mute,
in the cause of all who are left desolate.
Open your mouth, judge righteously,
and serve justice to the poor and needy."
Who can find a worthy woman?
For her value is far above rubies.
The heart of her husband trusts in her.
He shall have no lack of gain.

She does him good, and not harm,
all the days of her life.
She seeks wool and flax,
and works eagerly with her hands.
She is like the merchant ships.
She brings her bread from afar.
She rises also while it is yet night,
gives food to her household,
and portions for her servant girls.
She considers a field, and buys it.
With the fruit of her hands, she plants a vineyard.
She arms her waist with strength,
and makes her arms strong.
She perceives that her merchandise is profitable.
Her lamp doesn't go out by night.
She lays her hands to the distaff,
and her hands hold the spindle.
She opens her arms to the poor;
yes, she extends her hands to the needy.
She is not afraid of the snow for her household,
for all her household are clothed with scarlet.
She makes for herself carpets of tapestry.
Her clothing is fine linen and purple.
Her husband is respected in the gates,
when he sits among the elders of the land.
She makes linen garments and sells them,

and delivers sashes to the merchant.
Strength and dignity are her clothing.
She laughs at the time to come.
She opens her mouth with wisdom.
Kind instruction is on her tongue.
She looks well to the ways of her household,
and doesn't eat the bread of idleness.
Her children rise up and call her blessed.
Her husband also praises her:
"Many women do noble things,
but you excel them all."
Charm is deceitful, and beauty is vain;
but a woman who fears the LORD, she shall be praised.
Give her of the fruit of her hands!
Let her works praise her in the gates!

It also might be worth noting that even if the Proverbs 31 woman *was* an actual woman, much like many of the wealthy tradwife influencers, as a queen she would have resources not available to the average person.

As Bobbi Dempsey writes in her article *'We do not all "have as many hours as Beyonce"'*:

"Working-class folks don't have an entire troop of nannies, assistants, cleaning people, trainers, and

assorted other miscellaneous support staff who keep our lives running while freeing up large chunks in our schedule that we can then use for social activities and other luxuries."[42]

The next major movement that also shares hashtags and audience with the cottagecore aesthetic is homesteading, which often is summed up as the desire to get a little piece of land and live self-sufficiently. It brings to mind Thoreau in his cabin in the woods and Emerson's advocacy for living a natural and self-reliant life.

This doesn't seem nefarious in the slightest, but I also once joined a seed-sharing club thinking it was just about gardening only to find out it also had a doomsday-preppers undercurrent rooted in a cultish interpretation of the book of Revelations, so I find things often take surprising turns. Looking into the homesteading trend has been similarly surprising.

---

[42] Bobbi Dempsey, "We Do Not All 'Have as Many Hours as Beyoncé,'" *Quartz*, 13 Apr. 2018.

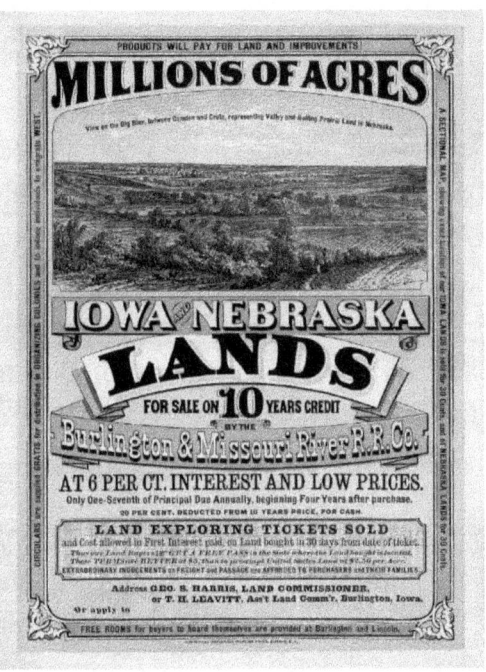

Figure 17 An advertisement for cheap undeveloped land, the colonial American dream!

The homesteading dream is actually deeply rooted in colonialism. In the USA it is another part of "The American Dream" influenced by The Homestead Act of 1862. This act was designed to develop the American West and promised 160 acres of land to anyone who would agree to farm it. A similar promise was made to Southerners with the Southern Homestead Act of 1866 and by 1890 more than 373,000 homesteads had been granted by the federal government on approximately 48 million acres of 'undeveloped' land.[43]

Similar offers were made across colonial countries and settlements wherever the need for cultural or economic advancement was seen as necessary or beneficial. In New Zealand history, land changed hands through various and sometimes very underhanded means which contributed to the New Zealand Wars between 1945 to 1872 and ongoing tensions which remain unresolved today.

Supreme Court rulings informed by colonial values viewed 'uncultivated' land as 'waste land' that belonged to the Crown, which was later addressed in the Native Land Acts of 1862 and 1865 which recognized Māori had rights to uncultivated land – although this was limited only if they had the certificate of title.[44] This caused further complications as traditional Māori concepts of land ownership were not exclusive – different family groups could have rights to the same land for different purposes at the same time. Yet when

---

[43] "Landmark Legislation: The Homestead Act of 1862." *The Civil War: The Senate's Story,* The United States Senate.
[44] Jim McAloon, *'Land ownership'*, Te Ara - the Encyclopedia of New Zealand, http://www.TeAra.govt.nz/en/land-ownership/print Accessed 4 November 2024.

applying for title, a limited number of names would have to go on the documentation and sales could be made by a single person who did not represent the interests of others who had traditional rights to the land.[45]

Peaceful protests by the ploughmen of Parihaka are a strong visual representation of a core issue with the colonial attitudes towards 'undeveloped land.' Under the leadership of Te Whiti o Rongomai and Tohu Kakahi in a movement for peace and independence, Māori men pushed ploughs across land throughout Taranaki, much of which had been claimed by the Crown and sold to settlers. This action spoke a loud message: *'You say we are not using this land, but see? We are using it.'*[46]

Across the world wherever colonization has occurred, you are likely to find harrowing stories of disenfranchisement which has ongoing effects today. The homesteading movement has had pushback online from critics who maintain that the dream of the 160-acre farm, the quarter-acre block,

---

[45] Ibid.
[46] *"Parihaka."* Te Ātiawa Iwi, https://teatiawa.iwi.nz/history/parihaka/ Accessed 4 Nov. 2024.

or whichever parcel of land is prominent in your country of choice, perpetuates the harms that colonization has wrought and stand in the way of decolonization discussions.

We find, as Frodo Baggins could attest, that even if you aim to live a quiet life away from the rest of the world, it doesn't mean the world ceases to exist. Even Thoreau, after his two years and two months at Walden, found it necessary to return to society. While we may each aim to cultivate our cozy homes and enjoy our own escapist dreams, it pays to keep one foot in reality.

I leave you with these small pieces of advice:

- Enjoy things, and let other people enjoy things too – even if those things are different to your own.
- Keep an eye on your relationship with technology and if you find yourself in too deep, take a break. Keep in mind that algorithms will push you to further extremes and you may need to recalibrate your preferences from time to time.
- Talk to people who are different from you, and you'll always have access to outside

perspectives. Cottagecore and its neighbouring communities can lead to isolating lifestyles, so make sure you don't get *too* isolated.
- It's fine to explore your identity, but don't give away your independence and ability to make choices permanently. They are hard won and easily lost.
- Remember cottagecore is meant to be an escapist dream but it is an unattainable reality by design, so limit your expectations and enjoy the small and incomplete things.

Want to find out more about the Language of Flowers? Check out my guide to floriography!

https://laurawolfbookclub.wordpress.com/the-flower-code/

Are you suffering from burnout or another condition with Chronic Pain and Fatigue?

I've compiled all my hard-won tips in this helpful book!
https://laurawolfbookclub.wordpress.com/chronic-pain-and-fatigue/

Need a cozy sweet romance book full of good vibes?

Check out my Billionaire Sweethearts series!

https://laurawolfbookclub.wordpress.com/books/

Thank you so much for purchasing this book.

The only reason I can afford to spend my time writing is due to you lovely readers. When I came down ill with chronic pain and fatigue, it was funds from my book royalties that paid for my ergonomic computer set up. I legitimately wasn't sure if I'd be able to continue, but you guys really came through for me.

When I've struggled with anxiety and wondering whether I even should continue, it's been the continued reviews and book sales that have kept me going – proof that people are still out there wanting to read what I've put together.

Thank you for your support. Seriously.

If you liked this book, please consider giving it a review and sharing it online – and maybe checking out some of my other titles!

Bibliography

Literature:

Anishanslin, Zara. *Portrait of a Woman in Silk: Hidden Histories of the British Atlantic World.* Yale University Press, 2016.

Austen, Jane. *Emma.* 1816.

Bavishi, A., M. D. Slade, and B. R. Levy. "A Chapter a Day: Association of Book Reading with Longevity." *Social Science & Medicine*, Sept. 2016.

Blackwell, Elizabeth. *A Curious Herbal.* Samuel Harding, 1737.

Britannica, The Editors of Encyclopaedia. "Nicolas Leblanc". *Encyclopedia Britannica*, 21 Mar. 2024, Accessed 1 November 2024.
https://www.britannica.com/biography/Nicolas-Leblanc.

Buskirk, Clarence Augustus. *A Cavern for a Hermitage.* New York, J. B. Alden, 1889.

Cadbury, Henry J. "George Fox". *Encyclopedia Britannica*, 27 Jun. 2024, Accessed 1 November 2024.
https://www.britannica.com/biography/George-Fox.

Caverley, C. S., translator. *Theocritus.* G. Bell, 1883. Available on microfilm. Kohler Collection of British Poetry.

Charmantier, Dr. Isabelle. "Linnaeus and Race." *The Linnean Society*, 3 Sept. 2020.
https://www.linnean.org/learning/who-was-linnaeus/linnaeus-and-race.

Chung, Erica, MPH. "Lead in Your Dishware?" *Center for*

Environmental Health, 23 Oct. 2018.

Crosby, Gillian. *First Impressions: The Prohibition on Printed Calicoes in France, 1686-1759*. Thesis, Nottingham Trent University, July 2015.

Da Vinci, Leonardo. *The Codex Arundel*. Circa 1480 – 1518.

Deardorff, Julie, and Karisa King. "Chicago Doctor's Research Fails Federal Smell Test." *Chicago Tribune*, 19 January 2014.

Dempsey, Bobbi. "We Do Not All 'Have as Many Hours as Beyoncé.'" *Quartz*, 13 Apr. 2018.

Ebrahimi, M., N. Khalili, S. Razi, M. Keshavarz-Fathi, N. Khalili, and N. Rezaei. "Effects of Lead and Cadmium on the Immune System and Cancer Progression." *Journal of Environmental Health Science & Engineering*, 17 Feb. 2020.

Emerson, R. W. *Nature*. Boston and Cambridge, James Munroe and Company, 1849.

"Garthwaite, Anna Maria." *English Heritage*, Accessed 1 Nov. 2024.
https://www.english-heritage.org.uk/.

George, Sam and Alison E. Martin. "Introduction: Botanising Women: Transmission, Translation and European Exchange." *Journal of Literature and Science,* vol. 4, no. 1, 2016.

Gilpin, William. *Observations on the River Wye, and Several Parts of South Wales, etc. Relative Chiefly to Picturesque Beauty; made in the Summer of the Year 1770.* London, Blamire, 1770.

Glass, Nancy, et al. "Non-Fatal Strangulation Is an Important

Risk Factor for Homicide of Women." *Journal of Emergency Medicine*, Oct. 2008.

Huecker, Martin R., Kevin C. King, Gary A. Jordan, and William Smock. "Domestic Violence." *StatPearls Publishing LLC*, 9 Apr. 2023. CC BY-NC-ND 4.0.

Lama, Dalai, Desmond Tutu, and Douglas Abrams. *The Book of Joy*. Hutchinson Publishing, 2016.

"Landmark Legislation: The Homestead Act of 1862." *The Civil War: The Senate's Story,* The United States Senate, Accessed 1 Nov. 2024.
https://www.senate.gov/artandhistory/history/common/civil_war/Homestead_Act.htm.

"Licensing the First US Patent." *Invention Stories*, The Lemelson Center: Smithsonian Institution, Accessed 1 Nov. 2024.
https://invention.si.edu/invention-stories/licensing-first-us-patent.

London, Bernard. *Ending the Depression Through Planned Obsolescence*. 1932.

McAloon, Jim. "Land Ownership." Te Ara - the Encyclopedia of New Zealand, http://www.TeAra.govt.nz/en/land-ownership/print. Accessed 4 Nov. 2024.

"Measuring Unpaid Domestic and Care Work." *International Labour Organization*, Accessed 1 Nov. 2024.
https://ilostat.ilo.org/topics/unpaid-work/measuring-unpaid-domestic-and-care-work/

Nakao, M. "Board Games as a Promising Tool for Health Promotion: A Review of Recent Literature." *Biopsychosocial*

Medicine, 19 Feb. 2019.

"Parihaka." Te Ātiawa Iwi. https://teatiawa.iwi.nz/history/parihaka/. Accessed 4 Nov. 2024.

PositivePulseQuotes. "Andrew Tate Quotes About Women." *Medium*, 16 Apr. 2024.

Prictor, Megan. "Millions of People's DNA in Doubt as 23andMe Faces Bankruptcy." *Science Alert*, 21 Oct. 2024.

"Psychiatry: The Wife Beater & His Wife." *Time*, 25 Sept. 1964.

Reagan, Romany. "The Language of Flowers: Breaking into the Boys Club of Botany & the Flowery Dress as a Feminist Act." *Blackthorn & Stone*, 2 July 2020.

Seaton, Beverly. *The Language of Flowers: A History*. University of Virginia Press, 1995.

Sutherland, Diane, Jon Sutherland, Liz Keevill, Kevin Eyres, and Maria Costantino. *Household Hints, Naturally: Garden, Beauty, Health, Cooking, Laundry, Cleaning*. New ed., Flame Tree Publishing, 1 Sept. 2019.

The Bible. World English Bible, Proverbs 31.

The Strangulation Training Institute, Accessed 1 Nov. 2024. https://www.strangulationtraininginstitute.com/

Thoreau, Henry David. *Walden; or, Life in the Woods*. Ticknor and Fields, 1854.

Travers, Brittany G., et al. "Knowing How to Fold 'em: Paper

Folding across Early Childhood." *Journal of Motor Learning and Development,* vol. 6, no. 1, June 2018.

Travers, Mark. "A Psychologist Explains the Dangers of the 'Tradwife' Movement." *Forbes,* 6 Jan. 2024.

van der Kolk, Bessel, M.D. *The Body Keeps the Score.* Penguin Books, 2015.

Ward, N. B. On the Growth of Plants in Closely Glazed Cases. 2nd ed., J. Van Voorst, 1852.

Images:
"Alcoa Aluminum Advert." 1953. Public domain, via Wikimedia Commons.

Blackwell, Elizabeth. "Garden Cucumber." *A Curious Herbal.* Samuel Harding, 1737.

"Chase & Sanborn Ad." *Life Magazine,* 11 Aug. 1952, p. 103.

"Dwight's Saleratus Trade Card." 1870. Boston Public Library.

Feke, Robert. "Anne Shippen Willing (Mrs. Charles Willing)." 1746.

Gadbois, Louis. "La Promenade de Napoleon au Hameau." 1811.

Hokusai, Katsushika. "Portrait of Matsuo Basho." 18th-19th century. Accessed via WikiMedia Commons 4 Nov. 2024.

Horenbout, Lucas. "Catherine of Aragon with a Monkey." Circa 1525-1526. Accessed via WikiMedia Commons 4 Nov. 2024.

"Millions of Acres Iowa and Nebraska Lands Advert." Burlington & Missouri River R. R. Co, 1872. Library of Congress Printed Ephemera Collection.

Peake, Robert, the Elder. *Lady in a Blackwork Petticoat.* Circa 1600. Yale Center for British Art, Paul Mellon Collection. Accessed via WikiMedia Commons 4 Nov. 2024.

"Sashiko Jacket." *Metropolitan Museum of Art*, CC0. Accessed via Wikimedia Commons 4 Nov. 2024.

"Sashiko Stitches." *Metropolitan Museum of Art*, CC0. Accessed via Wikimedia Commons 4 Nov. 2024.

"Statue of Sadako Sasaki." Sculpture by Hazel Reeves, Wikimedia Commons 4.0.

"Wardian Case." *On the Growth of Plants in Closely Glazed Cases*, 2nd ed., N. B. Ward, J. Van Voorst, 1852.

Wertmüller, Adolf Ulrik. "Queen Marie Antoinette of France and Two of Her Children Walking in The Park of Trianon." 1785.

Media:
Stevens, Cat. "Father and Son." *Tea for the Tillerman*, 1970. (Song).

Swift, Taylor. *Folklore*. 2020. (Album).

Taika Waititi. *Hunt for the Wilderpeople*. 2016. (Movie).

Woah Dude. "It Costs That Much." 2021. (Song).

@VBirchwood. *YouTube Channel*. YouTube.

www.ingramcontent.com/pod-product-compliance
Lightning Source LLC
Chambersburg PA
CBHW070528090426
42735CB00013B/2896